Understandings of the Church

Understandings of the Church

Everett Ferguson, volume editor;
George Kalantzis, series editor

Fortress Press
Minneapolis

UNDERSTANDINGS OF THE CHURCH

Cover image: Mosaic of church on the floor of the Church of the Holy Sepulcher, the traditional site of the crucifixion, burial, and resurrection of Jesus Christ/Ryan Rodrick Beiler/Shutterstock.com

Cover design: Laurie Ingram

Library of Congress Cataloging-in-Publication Data

Print ISBN: 978-1-4514-9636-9
eBook ISBN: 978-1-5064-1692-2

The paper used in this publication meets the minimum requirements of American National Standard for Information Sciences — Permanence of Paper for Printed Library Materials, ANSI Z329.48-1984.

Manufactured in the U.S.A.

This book was produced using Pressbooks.com, and PDF rendering was done by PrinceXML.

To the Southwest Seminar on the Development of Early Catholic Christianity, founded by Albert C. Outler and William R. Farmer in 1966 and still meeting. Intentionally ecumenical from the beginning, the Seminar has comprised members of various religious groups, including Cistercians from Our Lady of Dallas Abbey–David Balas (now deceased), Denis Farkasfalvy, and Roch Kereszty–among others. We learned from and taught one another.

Contents

Series Foreword

In his book *The Spirit of Early Christian Thought*, Robert Louis Wilken reminds us that "Christianity is more than a set of devotional practices and a moral code: it is also a way of thinking about God, about human beings, about the world and history."[1] From its earliest times, Wilken notes, Christianity has been inescapably ritualistic, uncompromisingly moral, and unapologetically intellectual.

Christianity is deeply rooted in history and continues to be nourished by the past. The ground of its being and the basis of its existence is the life of a historic person, Jesus of Nazareth, whom Christians identify as God's unique, historical act of self-communication. Jesus presented himself within the context of the history of the people of Israel, and the earliest disciples understood him to be the culmination of that history, ushering in a new chapter in God's ongoing engagement with the world.

The crucial period of the first few centuries of Christianity is known as the patristic era or the time of the church fathers. Beginning after the books of the New Testament were written and continuing until the dawn of the Middle Ages, this period

1. Robert Louis Wilken, *The Spirit of Early Christian Thought: Seeking the Face of God* (New Haven: Yale University Press, 2003), xiii.

(c. 100–700 CE) encompasses a large and diverse company of thinkers and personalities. Some came from Greece and Asia Minor, others from Palestine and Egypt, and still others from Spain, Italy, North Africa, Syria, and present-day Iraq. Some wrote in Greek, others in Latin, and others in Syriac, Coptic, Armenian, and other languages.

This is the period during which options of belief and practice were accepted or rejected. Christian teachers and thinkers forged the language to express Christian belief clearly and precisely; they oversaw the life of the Christian people in worship and communal structure; and they clarified and applied the worshiping community's moral norms.

Every generation of Christians that has reconsidered the adequacy of its practice and witness and has reflected seriously on what Christians confess and teach has come to recognize the church fathers as a precious inheritance and source for instruction and illumination. After the New Testament, no body of Christian literature has laid greater claim on Christians as a whole.

The purpose of this series is to invite readers "to return to the sources," to discover firsthand the riches of the common Christian tradition and to gain a deeper understanding of the faith and practices of early Christianity. When we recognize how Christian faith and practices developed through time, we also appreciate how Christianity still reflects the events, thought, and social conditions of this earlier history.

Ad Fontes: Sources of Early Christian Thought makes foundational texts accessible through modern, readable English translations and brief introductions that lay out the context of these documents. Each volume brings together the best recent scholarship on the topic and gives voice to varying points of view to illustrate the diversity of early Christian thought. Entire writings or sections of writings are provided to allow the reader to see the context and flow of the argument.

Together, these texts not only chronicle how Christian faith and practice came to adopt its basic shape but also summon contemporary readers to consider how the events, insights, and social conditions of the early church continue to inform Christianity in the twenty-first century.

George Kalantzis
Series Editor

1

Introduction

The study of ecclesiology often deals with the institutional, external aspects of the church. Less attention has been given to the nature or essence of the church. One approach many have found helpful in studying the essential nature of the church is by way of the images employed in reference to it.[1] Paul Minear demonstrated the value of this approach in regard to the New Testament in his impressive and influential compilation, *Images of the Church in the New Testament.*[2] Less attention,

1. This Introduction is adapted from a lecture I gave titled "Images of the Church in Early Christian Literature," which was published in Everett Ferguson, *The Early Church at Work and Worship*, vol. 1, *Ministry, Ordination, Covenant, and Canon* (Eugene, OR: Cascade, 2013), 1–14. This introduction forms part of my article, "Community and Worship," in D. Jeffrey Bingham, ed., *The Routledge Companion to Early Christian Thought* (London: Routledge, 2010), 313–30.
2. Paul Minear, *Images of the Church in the New Testament* (Philadelphia: Westminster, 1960). I covered the images used for the church in the New Testament in my book *The Church of Christ: A Biblical Ecclesiology for Today* (Grand Rapids: Eerdmans, 1996), chap. 2. H. Rikhof, *The Concept of the Church: A Methodological Inquiry into the Use of Metaphor in Ecclesiology* (London: Sheed & Ward, 1981), and Avery Dulles, *Models of the Church* (Garden City, NY: Doubleday, 1987), examined imagery in contemporary theological discussion of the church.

however, has been given to the use of images for the church in Christian writers of the early centuries after the New Testament. For example, Thomas Halton's collection of sources, *The Church,*[3] for the series Message of the Fathers of the Church (volume 4) gives only 10 out of 234 pages to the images of the church, noting the church as sheepfold, as edifice, as mother, as bride of Christ, and as the sheet let down from heaven in Peter's vision (Acts 10:9–16). Or again, E. Glenn Hinson in his nearly contemporary collection of sources, *Understandings of the Church,*[4] for the series Sources of Early Christian Thought, the predecessor of the present volume, gives no explicit treatment of images for the church.

While there have been studies devoted to the doctrine of the church in the early centuries,[5] some of which discuss images of the church,[6] the major contribution to the study of imagery for the church in early Christian literature is F. Ledegang, *Mysterium Ecclesiae: Images of the Church and its Members in Origen,*[7] a massive work of nearly seven hundred pages. Ledegang's comprehensive study groups the scores of images and related terminology in the writings of Origen (185–251) with its parallels in early Christian literature into six categories: body of Christ, bride of Christ, family, house and

3. Thomas Halton, *The Church*, Message of the Fathers of the Church (Wilmington, DE: Michael Glazier, 1985).

4. E. Glenn Hinson, *Understandings of the Church*, Sources of Early Christian Thought (Philadelphia: Fortress, 1986).

5. Gustav Bardy wrote *La théologie de l'Église de Clément de Rom au saint Irénée* (Paris: Cerf, 1945) and *La théologie de l'Église de saint Irénée au concile de Nicée* (Paris: Cerf, 1947). Ladislas Spikowski had earlier written his doctoral dissertation titled *La doctrin de l'Église dans Saint Irénée* (Strasbourg: Université de Strasbourg, 1926).

6. Hugo Rahner, *Symbole der Kirche: Die Ekklesiologie der Väter* (Salzburg: Otto Müller, 1964). David Rankin (*Tertullian and the Church* [Cambridge University Press, 1995]) devoted twenty-six pages to "Tertullian's ecclesiastical images," and G. G. Christo wrote a dissertation titled *The Church's Identity Established through Images according to Saint John Chrysostom* (Rolli, NH: Orthodox Research Institute, 2006).

7. F. Ledegang, *Mysterium Ecclesiae: Images of the Church and its Members in Origen* (Leuven: Leuven University Press, 2001).

sanctuary, people of God, and "the earth and all that is in it." I will take Ledegang's six categories as the framework for my further introductory remarks. For the most part, I will take those images with a basis in the New Testament but then note an additional one.

What is immediately evident in these images for the church is that they all emphasize the *communal* aspect of Christian faith and life. This communal emphasis stands in contrast to the individualistic approach of so many of the expressions of Christianity in the modern Western world. Most of these images are rooted in biblical usage. They furthermore testify not only to the importance of the church in Christian thought but also to the relation of the church to key theological concepts.

Body of Christ

Paul's image of the church as the body of Christ has remained popular throughout Christian history. He used the analogy to emphasize unity along with diversity in Christian congregations in Rom 12:4–8 and especially 1 Cor 12:12–27, where Christ is the whole body and Christians are members of him. The imagery shifts in the later epistles, where in Col 1:18 Christ is the head of the body in the sense of origin or source of the whole church, and in Eph 1:21–23 Christ is the head of the body in the sense of authority over the universal church.

The use of the imagery of the church as the body of Christ occurs early in Christian literature outside the New Testament. One of the earliest noncanonical Christian writings (perhaps 96 CE), the letter of the "church of God in Rome to the church of God in Corinth," rightly it seems ascribed to Clement of Rome and now known as *1 Clement*, clearly alludes to 1 Cor 12:14–26 in its appeal for unity in the church at Corinth, once again troubled with division.[8]

The homily we know as *2 Clement* (early to mid-second century), wrongly ascribed to Clement of Rome, employed the language of the church as the body of Christ in order to affirm the preexistence of the church. As Christ is preexistent, so is his body. In stressing the close identification of the church with Christ, the author takes the body as the equivalent of the flesh of Christ. The result is an implicit argument against a docetic/gnostic disparagement of the flesh.[9] Hermas, a prophet in the first half of the second century in Rome, similarly says that the church was created first of all things.[10]

Clement of Alexandria (d. c. 215) also made use of the body imagery for the church. In commenting on Ps 19:4–6, he quotes some who say that the "Lord's tabernacle is his body," but others say, "it is the church of the faithful."[11] Instead of moving from Christ to the church, as did *2 Clement*, Clement of Alexandria uses this imagery of the church as the body of Christ to reason back to the nature of Christ. He alludes to 1 Cor 12:12 with the words, "As a human being consisting of many members . . . is a combination of two—a body of faith and a soul of hope—so the Lord is of flesh and blood."[12] In an extended commentary on 1 Corinthians 6, Clement applies the language of body to the church; with special reference to verse 13 he says,

> The church of the Lord is figuratively speaking a body, the spiritual and holy chorus. Those who have been only called these things, but do not live according to the word, are fleshly. "But

8. *1 Clem.* 37.5.
9. *2 Clem.* 14.2–4.
10. *Herm. Vis.* 2.4 [8].
11. Clement of Alexandria, *Prophetic Eclogues* 56.
12. Clement of Alexandria, *Instructor* 1.6.42.

> this spiritual body," that is the holy church, "is not for fornication."[13] It is not fitting in any manner, however little, to abandon the gospel for the pagan life.[14]

Here like *2 Clement* as well as other authors, for Clement of Alexandria the church as the body of Christ has important implications for the manner of life of its members.

Origen made extensive use of the body imagery for the church. He picked up on the universal use of the image of the church as the body of Christ in the later Pauline letters but blended it with the language of Paul's earlier use for individual members. Like Clement of Alexandria before him, Origen uses this imagery of the body of Christ to reason back to the nature of Christ. In the context of our quotation in the section on Origen from *Against Celsus* 6.48, Origen uses the analogy of the church to a body, animated by a soul, to support the union of the soul of Jesus, perfect man, with the eternal Word, Son of God; but he is drawing on 1 Cor 12:12 and 27 and Rom 12:4–5.

Paul's image of the church as body of Christ must have worked itself into the Christian consciousness for it to be used so early, not only for a similar purpose as Paul's in *1 Clement*'s call to unity, but also for such different purposes from Paul's as to argue for the nature of Christ (Clement of Alexandria and Origen) and for the preexistence of the church (*2 Clement*) as well as against sexual immorality (*2 Clement* and Clement of Alexandria).

Bride of Christ

Another picture of the close, intimate relationship of the church to Christ given by Paul is that of the bride of Christ.

13. An allusion to 1 Cor 6:13.
14. Clement of Alexandria, *Miscellanies* 7.14.87.3. Cf. *Instructor* 1.5.22, "Believers are members of Christ."

This image has Old Testament precedent of God as a husband to Israel.[15] Paul employed the bridal imagery to stress the church's purity.[16] The seer John used bridal imagery to express the expectation of the eschatological consummation of the church's union with Christ.[17] The bride is a corporate image, but as we'll see, some made it a personal image for an individual soul.

Clement of Alexandria applied the purity of the bride to the church avoiding heresies. He interpreted Rom 7:2, 4, to mean Christians belong to Christ as "bride and church, which must be pure both from inner thoughts contrary to the truth and from outward temptations," which he identifies as heresies.[18]

Tertullian (c. 160–220) stressed that the church as a bride comes to Christ as a virgin. Against the proclamation by a bishop (whether in Rome or in Carthage is not clear) of forgiveness for the sins of adultery and fornication, the rigorist Tertullian, who considered these sins unforgiveable by the church, protested, "The church is a virgin! Far from Christ's betrothed be such a proclamation."[19] On the church as a virgin, note also *On Modesty* 18.11 and *On Monogamy* 11.2, "virgin church betrothed to the one Christ," and *Against Marcion* 5.12.6. The church as bride of Christ occurs in other passages as well.[20]

Origen applied the imagery of the bride to the church in his *Commentary on the Song of Songs*. He connected the language of body with that of a bride. Commenting on Paul's words, "Our bodies are members of Christ," he explained, "for when he says 'our bodies,' he shows that these bodies are the body of the bride; but when he mentions the 'members of Christ,'

15. Jer 2:2; Ezek 16:8–14; Hos 2:1–3:1.
16. 2 Cor 11:2.
17. Rev 19:7–8; 21:2, 9.
18. Clement of Alexandria, *Miscellanies* 3.12.80.
19. Tertullian, *On Modesty* 1.8.
20. Tertullian, *On Monogamy* 5.7 and *Against Marcion* 4.11.8; 5.18.9.

he indicates that these same bodies are the body of the Bridegroom."[21] The words addressed by the Bridegroom to the bride in Song of Songs, Origen says, are "words spoken by Christ to the church."[22] They "can be understood as spoken of this present age, for even now the church is fair when she is near to Christ and imitates Christ."[23] Origen anticipated later individualistic spirituality in also applying the bridal imagery to the individual soul, but it should be noted that for Origen the individual soul does not establish a bridal relationship in her own right apart from the church. The soul becomes bride only as it enters into the church's bridal relationship to Christ. The same could be said for others who make the same move to the individual soul. Origen writes: "The blessed soul burns and is aflame and sings that marriage song through the Spirit by which the church is joined to her heavenly spouse, Christ."[24]

The bridal imagery was especially used to emphasize the purity of the church. Methodius (d. c. 311) was a critic of Origen on some points of doctrine, but he shared with him the image of church as bride. In his *Symposium*, or the *Banquet of the Ten Virgins*, Methodius says that those who embrace the truth and are delivered from the evils of the flesh become "a church and help-meet of Christ, betrothed and given in marriage to him as a virgin, according to the apostle."[25]

Mother

The most important aspect of family imagery for the church in early Christianity was that of the mother. The image of the church as mother was one of the most popular in early

21. Origen, *Commentary on the Song of Songs* 3.2 on 1:16.
22. Ibid., 3.15 on 2:13–14.
23. Ibid., 3.1 on 1:15.
24. Ibid., prologue 2.
25. Methodius, *Banquet of the Ten Virgins* 3.8.74; cf. 2 Cor 11:2.

Christianity, for which there is a comprehensive study by Joseph C. Plumpe, *Mater Ecclesia: An Inquiry into the Concept of the Church as Mother in Early Christianity*.[26]

This image of the church is not so prominent in the New Testament, but there are anticipations of it. Paul in his allegory of Hagar and Sarah says Sarah "corresponds to the Jerusalem above; . . . she is our mother."[27] The book of Revelation's vision in chapter 12 of the woman who gave birth to the Messiah and also to other children and who was persecuted by the dragon represents by her the people of God including the church.

Irenaeus (fl. c. late second century) in his catechetical work *Demonstration* [or *Proof*] *of the Apostolic Preaching* 94 uses the language of motherhood to contrast the church and the synagogue: "The Lord grants more children to the church than to the synagogue of the past." In chapter 98, he says that the church throughout the world hands down the preaching of the truth to her children. Elsewhere Irenaeus says against heretics that those "who do not partake of the Spirit [of God] are not nourished into life from the mother's breasts."[28]

The *Letter of the Churches of Lyons and Vienne* (c. 177) provides one of the early uses of maternal imagery for the church. When Christians denied the faith under persecution, others in the church mourned as for children whom she had miscarried; but, when some of those who denied returned to the faith, the church, described as a "virgin mother," "rejoiced at their being made alive again."[29]

Clement of Alexandria too used the paradox of virgin mother for the church.[30] As a mother the church draws

26. Joseph C. Plumpe, *Mater Ecclesia: An Inquiry into the Concept of the Church as Mother in Early Christianity* (Washington, DC: Catholic University of America Press, 1943).
27. Gal 4:26.
28. Irenaeus, *Against Heresies* 3.24.1.
29. Eusebius, *Church History* 5.1.45; cf. 5.1.49.
30. Clement of Alexandria, *Instructor* 1.6.42.1.

children to herself,[31] and the members as children seeking the church "run to our good mother."[32] Family imagery is a favorite with Clement, and he frequently refers to Christians as children.

Tertullian made frequent use of the imagery of the church as mother, as I note in the quotations from him. The statement in Galatians 4:26 that the "Jerusalem above" "is our mother" prompted the comment that this is "the holy church in whom we have expressed our faith."[33] One scholar takes this not as Tertullian's comment but as part of his quotation from Marcion,[34] who thus becomes the first to call the church mother, but the language sounds to me more like Tertullian's.

When Origen employed the image of mother for the church, he was precise that the origin of Christians is with God the Father and not with the church. It is through the mother that God begets sons and daughters. Others were not always so careful and sometimes spoke as if the children (Christians) derived from the church; probably if pressed they too would have acknowledged the theological priority of God.

Latin Christianity's fondness for the imagery of church as mother is seen in Cyprian (d. 258), who refers to the church as mother more than thirty times.[35] For instance, in his reasoning against accepting baptism performed by heretics he makes the following argument: "The Spirit cannot be received, unless he who receives it first exists. [His point is that one cannot receive the Spirit until first being reborn in the church.] This being so, where and of what mother to whom is he born who is not a son of the church? If one is to have God as his Father, he must first

31. Ibid., 1.5.19.
32. Ibid., 3.12.99.
33. Tertullian, *Against Marcion* 5.4.8.
34. Ledegang, *Mysterium Ecclesiae*, 206.
35. Plumpe, *Mater Ecclesia*, 81.

have the church for a mother."[36] This is similar to his famous declaration against schism: "He can no longer have God for his Father who has not the church for his mother."[37]

Methodius in the same section on the church as bride[38] used the imagery of motherhood for the church. Like Origen, he was careful not to ascribe the generating power to the mother, but unlike Origen he ascribed the implanting of the spiritual seed to Christ and not to God.[39]

Rhetorically perceptive thinkers were alert to the parallel paradoxes of the church as virgin bride and mother and of Mary as virgin and mother of Jesus. Augustine (354–430) later succinctly expressed the idea: "The church, imitating the Mother of God [Mary] . . . is both mother and virgin."[40] This led to the view of Mary as a personification of the church, but that is a development largely outside the time frame of this collection of sources.

Building/Temple

The architectural image of the church as a building most often is that of a temple. The New Testament basis of this imagery is abundant. Paul addressing the church in Corinth said, "You are God's building."[41] He followed with the statement, "Do you not know that you are God's temple and that God's Spirit dwells in you."[42] Ephesians 2:19–22 elaborated on Christians as a "holy temple in the Lord," "a dwelling place for God," "built upon the foundation of the apostles and prophets, with Christ Jesus

36. *Letters* 74.7.2.
37. Cyprian, *On the Unity of the Church* 6.
38. *Symposium* 3.8.70–71.
39. Ibid., 3.8.70, 74; 8.8.190–91.
40. *Sermon* 191.3.
41. 1 Cor 3:9.
42. 1 Cor 3:16.

himself as the cornerstone." First Peter 2:4–5 speaks of the "spiritual house," of which Christians are "living stones" and in which they are a "holy priesthood," serving Jesus the "living Stone."

In the *Shepherd* of Hermas (first half of the second century), one of the Apostolic Fathers, the church as a whole is the building, but this time it is a tower and not a temple. In the elaborate parable of the tower in the *Similitudes*, "the rock and the door [or gate] are the Son of God."[43] "The tower is the church," and the stones placed in the building are those who take the name of the Son of God and are clothed with the appropriate virtues.[44] In Hermas's *Visions* that open the *Shepherd* it is also stated that "the tower that you see being built is the church," with the further comment that "the tower is built upon the waters" of baptism and "is founded on the word of the almighty and glorious name."[45]

Early in Christian literature the *Epistle of Barnabas* (late first–early second century CE) expressed the theme of the spiritual temple replacing the physical temple in Jerusalem, but the author applied the idea only to the individual. The temple of the Lord is gloriously built when "having received the forgiveness of sins and having placed hope in his name, we became new." "Therefore God truly resides in our dwelling place."[46]

Clement of Alexandria repeated the argument of early Christian apologists against material temples, while applying the terminology of temple to the church and the assembly of God's people. "Is it not the case that we do not rightly and truly circumscribe in any place the one who cannot be contained,

43. *Herm. Sim.* 9.12.1 [89].
44. Ibid., 9.13.1 [89]; 9.13.4–15.6 [90–92].
45. *Herm. Vis.* 3.3.3 and 5 [11].
46. *Barn.* 16.8; the whole chapter is relevant.

nor do we confine in temples made with hands that which contains all things? What work of builders, stone cutters, and of handicraft can be holy?"[47] He continued with the affirmation that the church is holy but is not a place, as was true of pagan temples and the Jewish temple, but is the assembly of God's chosen people. So, for Clement, in accord with the New Testament, God's temple now is not a building but the people assembled, as in the meaning of the Greek word for church, *ekklēsia*. In addition to the church, Clement used temple imagery for the cosmos, the soul of the true gnostic, the human body, and the body of Jesus.[48]

Tertullian has frequent use of motifs associated with a temple. For him Christ, in contrast to the Jewish temple that was destroyed, "is the true temple of God."[49] In *Against Marcion* 3.24 Christ is "the temple of God, and also the gate by whom heaven is entered." By extension Christians are "priests of the spiritual temple, that is of the church."[50] Alternatively, Christ was the rejected stone that became "the chief cornerstone," "accepted and elevated to the top place of the temple, even his church."[51] Tertullian thus reflects the varied applications in Scripture according to which Christ can be pictured as the temple and as the foundation of the temple. According to one use of the imagery, it is the Holy Spirit who builds "the church, which is indeed the temple, household, and city of God."[52] The church as the spiritual temple can also be said, following one interpretation of a New Testament text, to be built on Peter.[53]

47. Clement of Alexandria, *Miscellanies* 7.5.28.
48. Ledegang, *Mysterium Ecclesiae*, 320.
49. Tertullian, *Against the Jews* 13.15.
50. Ibid., 14.9.
51. Tertullian, *Against Marcion* 3.7.
52. Ibid., 3.23.
53. Tertullian, *On Monogamy* 8.

Individual Christians are themselves "temples of God, and altars, and lights, and sacred vessels."[54]

Origen could speak of the church as a house, but since the word "house" was often applied to a temple as the house of a deity, there could be overtones of a sacred house even in this usage. Origen stated that "the church is the house of the Son of God." And again, "The church or the churches, then, are the houses of the Bridegroom and the bride, the houses of the soul and the Word."[55]

Origen applied the specific language of a temple to the church mostly in biblical passages about the temple. His commentary on John 2:13–17 includes these words: "Jesus always finds some such [money changers] in the temple. For in what we call the church, which is the house 'of the living God, the pillar and ground of the truth,'[56] when are there not some money-changers sitting?"[57] The continuation of the passage in John 2:19–21 prompted Origen to combine the images of body and of temple, as does the Gospel of John, for the church:

> If the body of Jesus is said to be his temple, it is worth asking whether we must take this in a singular manner, or must endeavor to refer each of the things recorded about the temple anagogically to the saying about the body of Jesus, whether it be the body which he received from the virgin, or the church, which is said to be his body. . . .
>
> Someone . . . will say that the body, understood in either way, has been called the temple because as the temple had the glory of God dwelling in it, so the Firstborn of all creation, being the image and glory of God, is properly said to be the temple bearing the image of God in respect to his body or the church. . . .

54. Tertullian, *On the Crown* 9.
55. Origen, *Commentary on the Song of Songs* 3.3 on Song 1:17.
56. 1 Tim 3:15.
57. Origen, *Commentary on John* 10.23 (16).134.

> We shall attempt, however, to refer each of the statements that have reference to the temple anagogically to the church. . . .
>
> Then each of the living stones will be a stone of the temple according to the worth of its life here.[58]

Here, as is usual with him, Origen quickly moves from the corporate use of the image to the individual believer. The biblical material offered a rich lode from which Origen could mine moral and spiritual teachings.

People of God/Nation

The theme of the people of God represents one of the many continuities between the Old Testament and New Testament, where the language of the Old Testament is taken over for the church. I include here the terminology of nation or race in addition to people, for the words are often used almost interchangeably.[59] When God established his covenant with Israel at Mount Sinai, he said, "You shall be my treasured possession out of all the peoples. . . . You shall be for me a priestly kingdom and a holy nation."[60] The twin expressions "I am your God" and "You are my people" or their equivalent became a covenant formula.[61] First Peter 2:9–10 appropriates the Exodus passage for the church, and 2 Cor 6:16 takes over the language of the covenant formula.

Early apologists presented Christians as a third (or fourth) race. The *Epistle to Diognetus* says that Christians in their religion "neither acknowledge those considered to be gods by the Greeks nor observe the superstition of the Jews," but are a

58. Origen, *Commentary on John* 10.39 (23).263–64, 267–68.
59. D. K. Buell, *Why This New Race: Ethnic Reasoning in Early Christianity* (New York: Columbia University Press, 2005).
60. Exod 19:5–6.
61. Deut 26:17–18; 29:12–13; Jer 7:23; 11:4; 24:7; 31:33; Hos 2:23.

"new race or way of life."[62] The *Preaching of Peter* similarly says, "Do not worship as the Greeks," "neither worship as the Jews," but "worship in a new way by Christ."[63] Aristides argues as follows: "It is evident to us, O King, that there are three classes of people in this world: the worshipers of those called gods by you, the Jews, and the Christians." The Syriac version gives four by dividing the worshipers of other gods into barbarians and Greeks to go with the Jews and Christians.[64]

Justin Martyr (mid-second century) used the language of people and race in reference to the church in succession to Israel: "After that Righteous One was put to death, we flourished as another people." He continues, "We are not only a people but also a holy people" and a people chosen by God.[65] He continues by quoting Old Testament passages to show that the church of the Gentiles is a new Israel, "counted worthy to be called a people."[66] He further affirms that Christians are a high priestly race.[67]

Clement of Alexandria, in an extended discussion of different images for the children of God, says that the Lord "calls us sometimes children, sometimes chickens, sometimes infants, and at other times sons and often little children, and a new people and a recent people."[68] Without expressly using the word "church," Clement implied it in the language of a people. He made the contrast, "the old race [Israel] was perverse and hard hearted," but "we the new people are tender as a child."[69] "Formerly the older people had an older covenant, and the

62. *Epistle to Diognetus* 1.
63. Quoted by Clement of Alexandria, *Miscellanies* 6.5.
64. Aristides, *Apology* 2.
65. Justin Martyr, *Dialogue with Trypho* 119.3–4.
66. Ibid., 123.1.
67. Ibid., 116.3.
68. Clement of Alexandria, *Instructor* 1.5.14.
69. Ibid., 1.5.19.4.

law disciplined the people with fear, . . . but to the new and recent people a new covenant has been given, the Word has become flesh, and fear is turned into love."[70] The children of God "become a new, holy people, by regeneration."[71]

Alongside the word "people," Clement also used the word "race" for Christians. Out of the Greek and Jewish peoples "there are gathered into one race of the saved people those who come to faith."[72]

Tertullian too developed the theme of the two peoples. He interpreted Gen 25:23 about the two nations and two peoples in the womb of Rebekah as referring to the older people of Israel (the Jews) and the later or lesser people, the Christians.[73] In all the nations now "dwells the people of the name of Christ."[74] Unlike some of his predecessors, Tertullian rejected the designation "third race" for Christians and assigned its use to pagan critics.[75]

Origen worked with the theme of peoplehood quite extensively and in various ways. I select only one passage as illustrative of his approach. After contrasting the Egyptian people and the Israelite people and their respective priests, Origen addresses the congregation:

> Examine yourself and consider to which people you belong and the priesthood of which order you hold. If you still serve the carnal senses . . . know that you are of the Egyptian people. But if you have before your eyes the Decalogue of the law and the decade of the New Testament . . . and from that you offer tithes . . . "you are a true Israelite in whom there is no guile."[76]

70. Clement of Alexandria, *Instructor* 1.7.59.1.
71. Ibid., 1.6.32.4.
72. Clement of Alexandria, *Miscellanies* 6.5.42.
73. Tertullian, *Against the Jews* 1.
74. Ibid., 7.
75. Tertullian, *To the Nations* 8.
76. Quoting John 1:47. Origen, *Homilies on Genesis* 16.6.

Here as elsewhere Origen identifies the true Christian people with the true Israel of Old Testament Scripture.

Boat/Ark

Among the images drawn from nature and objects in the world, a boat, or especially the ark, is prominent. Here we come to imagery without explicit New Testament basis for the church, although there is a reference to the ark of Noah in 1 Pet 3:20.

The earliest reference to a ship other than the ark as the church appears to be Tertullian, *On Baptism* 12. He was responding to those who suggested that "the apostles underwent a substitute for baptism when in the little ship they were engulfed by the waves." Tertullian replied that this event was different from being "baptized by the rule of religion," and he then affirmed "that little ship presented a type of the church, because on the sea, which means this present world, it is being tossed about by the waves, which mean persecutions and temptations."

Some writers made imaginative comparisons between a ship and the church. The two most elaborate developments of the image—Hippolytus (first third of the third century), *On Christ and Antichrist* 59, and Pseudo-Clement (third century), *Letter of Clement to James* 14—are included in our selections. Although there are a few elements in common, for the most part the imagery is developed quite differently. One difference is that if one continues reading the passage from Pseudo-Clement, the following chapter applies the comparison to a ship by giving specific exhortations to the different members of the church.

It is notable that one common feature, where there are such different developments of the image of a ship in Hippolytus, Pseudo-Clement, and Tertullian as well, is that the sea is likened by all three to the world and the dangers it presents. Such imagery could go back to a lost apocalyptic book. Such is the suggestion of Erik Peterson, who has argued that the ship as a symbol of the church is a recasting of an older conception of Israel in an eschatological storm at sea.[77]

Although the Bible did not use the analogy of a ship to the church, the story of the ark of Noah gave a scriptural basis for an ecclesiological application, not itself developed in the Bible.

Latin Christianity made much use of the analogy of the ark and the church. Callistus, bishop of Rome, argued that "the ark of Noah was a symbol of the church, in which were both dogs, wolves, and ravens," and so he alleged that those guilty of sin, when forgiven, could remain in the church.[78] Tertullian alluded to this argument, referring to the different kinds of animals (raven, kite, dog, and serpent) in the ark as representing different types of persons in the church, but he insisted that no idolater was in the ark, so "let there not be in the church what was not in the ark."[79] He had already anticipated the theme of the ark as a type of the church in his treatment of the flood in Noah's day as a type of baptism. "The dove is the Holy Spirit, sent forth from heaven, where is the church, a figure of the ark."[80]

Origen was the first to work out the ark motif extensively in an ecclesiological sense. In his *Homilies on Genesis* he draws lessons for the church from the instructions about the building of the ark. "This people, therefore, which is saved in the church, is compared to all those whether men or animals that are saved in the ark."[81] He continues by interpreting the

77. Erik Peterson, "Das Schiff als Symbol der Kirche: Die Tat des Messias im eschatologischen Meerssturm in der jüdischen und altchristlichen Ueberlieferung," *Theologische Zeitschrift* 6 (1950): 77–79.
78. According to Hippolytus, *Refutation of All Heresies* 9.12 (7).23.
79. Tertullian, *On Idolatry* 24.4.
80. Tertullian, *On Baptism* 8.4.

different levels in the ark as degrees of progress in faith, and he takes Noah as an image of Christ. "Therefore, Christ, the spiritual Noah, in his ark in which he frees the human race from destruction, that is, in his church, has established in its breadth the number fifty, the number of forgiveness."[82] Fifty had the significance of forgiveness from the Year of Jubilee and its release from debts. This association of the ark with salvation goes back to 1 Pet 3:20–22 and was extensively employed in the early church, for which note Justin, *Dialogue with Trypho* 138; but Origen explicitly connects the ark with the church.

Cyprian, like his Latin-speaking predecessors, argued from the ark as a type of the church: 1 Pet 3:20–21 proves that "the one ark of Noah was a type of the one church," and so only the baptism administered in the church (and not by schismatics) is valid; on this analogy those outside the church will perish.[83] Thereafter the analogy of the ark and the church was common.

Implications

This sampling of the rich variety of early Christian imagery for the church demonstrates the importance of the church in the experience and practice of early Christians. The Christian life was a corporate life, lived in community with other believers. Thinking about the church, furthermore, was rooted in scriptural usage. The images emphasized the close association of the church with Christ and the Holy Spirit, the continuity with and progress from the Old Testament, the unity and spirituality of the church. The church was related to important doctrines—such as the nature of Christ and human salvation—and membership in the church was significant for

81. Origen, *Homilies on Genesis* 2.3.
82. Ibid., 2.5.
83. Cyprian, *Letters* 69.2.2; 75.15.

Christian character (holiness and purity). The lessons drawn by the early Christian authors may not always be applicable to today, but these "sources of early Christian thought" serve to enrich the "understandings of the church" that continue to challenge Christian thought.

Translation

Where credits are not given, the translations are my own.

2

1 Clement

The work known as *1 Clement* is actually a letter from "the church of God that resides in Rome to the church of God that resides in Corinth."[1] The actual author was early said, probably correctly, to be Clement, one of the bishops of Rome. The date of the letter was probably in the closing years of the decade of the 90s of the first century. The occasion for the letter was once more a matter of division in the church at Corinth, a problem addressed in Paul's first letter to the Corinthian church, only this time the problem was specifically the removal of some of the elders at the instigation of the younger members of the congregation. Their motive is not stated, although modern scholars offer several speculations. Clues within the letter do not go beyond an assumed spirit of jealousy and rebellion. The letter appeals to Paul's analogy of the church to the human body of many members, each necessary for the harmonious

1. *1 Clement* prologue.

working of the whole.[2] The following passages are valuable for their testimony to the early organizational structure of the church and testimony that this was of divine and apostolic origin. *First Clement* agrees with other early sources that each congregation was led by a plurality of those called presbyters (elders) or bishops (used interchangeably in the second passage) assisted by deacons (contrast Ignatius, below). The second passage makes incidental reference to the image of the local church as a flock of sheep belonging to Christ.

1 Clement 42.1–5

42.1–5. The apostles were given the gospel for us from the Lord Jesus Christ; Jesus the Christ was sent from God. 2. Christ therefore is from God, and the apostles are from Christ. They both, therefore, came in good order from the will of God. 3. When they received his commands, were fully convinced by the resurrection of our Lord Jesus Christ, and having placed their faith in the word of God, the apostles went out with the full assurance of the Holy Spirit, preaching the gospel that the kingdom of God is about to come. 4. They preached in every district and every city, and they appointed their first converts, after testing them by the Spirit, as bishops and deacons of those who were going to believe. 5. . . . For thus the Scripture says somewhere, "I will appoint their bishops in righteousness and their deacons in faith."[3]

1 Clement 44.1–6

44.1–6. Our apostles knew through our Lord Jesus Christ that

2. *1 Clem.* 37.5.
3. An otherwise unattested reading of Isa 60:17, which in the Greek says, "I will give your rulers in peace and your bishops [overseers] in righteousness."

there would be strife concerning the name of the episcopate. 2. For this reason, therefore, and having received perfect foreknowledge, they appointed those we mentioned above, and afterward they gave the rule that if these should die, other tested men should succeed to their ministry. 3. The men, therefore, who have been appointed by the apostles or afterward by other eminent men with the consent of the whole church and who have ministered blamelessly to the flock of Christ humbly, quietly, and unselfishly, men who have been well testified to by all for many years—these men we do not consider it just to expel from their ministry. 4. For it will be no small sin to us if we expel from the episcopate those who have offered the gifts blamelessly and in a holy manner. 5. Blessed are those presbyters who have died previously and had a fruitful and perfect departure. For they have no fear that someone will remove them from their established place. 6. For we see that you have removed some who have conducted themselves well from the ministry that has been blamelessly distinguished by them.

3

2 Clement

The work known as *2 Clement* is a hortatory sermon on repentance that in its transmission was incorrectly ascribed to Clement of Rome. It may have originated in Rome, Corinth, or Alexandria; its date is uncertain, perhaps the early or mid-second century. The author, perhaps distinct from the presbyters to whom he refers (17.3, 5), read his exhortation (19.1) following the Scripture reading, which at least included Isa 54:1, interpreted of the church, once barren but now bearing children (2.1). The reference to "the books and the apostles" refers to the Jewish Scriptures and the teachings and/or writings of the apostles. Notable ideas about the church are its existence before creation in the mind or plan of God but like Christ revealed in the new era; its association with life, the Spirit, salvation, and the Lord's election; and its identification as the body of Christ with his flesh along with the accompanying obligations for the kind of life lived in the flesh.[1]

2 Clement 14.1–5

14.1–5. So then, brothers and sisters, if we do the will of God our Father, we will belong to the first church, the spiritual church, which was created before the sun and moon. But if we do not do the will of the Lord, we will belong to those of whom the Scripture says, "My house has become a robbers' cave."[2] So then, let us choose to belong to the church of life in order that we may be saved. 2. I do not suppose you to be ignorant that the living church is the body of Christ, for the Scripture says, "God made the human being male and female."[3] The male is Christ; the female is the church. And you are not ignorant that the books and the apostles say that the church exists not only in the present but also from the beginning. For she was spiritual, as was also our Jesus, but she was manifested in the last days in order that she might save us. 3. Although the church was spiritual, she was manifested in the flesh of Christ, making clear to us that if anyone of us should guard her and not corrupt her in the flesh, he will receive her back in the Holy Spirit. For this flesh is a copy of the Spirit. Therefore, no one who corrupts the copy will receive the original. Hence, brothers and sisters, this means, "Guard the flesh so that you may receive the Spirit." 4. If we say that the flesh is the church and the Spirit is Christ, then, therefore, the person who abuses the flesh abuses the church. Such a person, therefore, will not receive the Spirit, which is Christ. 5. This flesh is capable of receiving such an incorruptible life, if the Holy Spirit clings to it. Nor is one able to express or tell what the Lord has prepared for his chosen ones.

1. See *2 Clem.* 9.1–5.
2. Jer 7:11; Matt 21:13.
3. Gen 1:27.

4

Ignatius of Antioch

Ignatius was bishop of Antioch during the reign of Emperor Trajan (ruled 98–117). Arrested for resisting the imperial cult, he was taken under armed escort to Rome, where he became a martyr for his faith in Christ. On his way across Asia Minor, he wrote letters to six churches and a letter to Polycarp of Smyrna. In these letters, he opposed Jewish practices as observed by Gentile Christians and especially the view that Jesus only appeared to have a human body with its accompanying disparagement of things material. Ignatius advocated unity against the divisions accompanying these practices and obedience to the ministry of the church as the means of achieving this unity. Obedience to a higher authority as the way to maintain unity has a long history in Christian practice but with dubious results. Ignatius championed the threefold ministry of one bishop, a plurality of presbyters, and deacons in each church, a pattern for which he is the first witness but which came to prevail in the second century. Ignatius indicates that the assembly, Eucharist, love feast, and baptism were important congregational activities. All church functions were to be conducted by the bishop or by someone he designated. Ignatius reflects themes from the writings of both Paul and John in the New Testament, including the ideas of being members of the body of Christ and particularly the emphasis on unity. Although the musical analogy for unity is common, Ignatius's elaboration of it for unity with the bishop is distinctive. Similarly he puts his own stamp on the use of temple and sacrificial imagery for the church.

Ephesians 4–6

4.1. Hence it is proper for you to live together in harmony with the mind of the bishop, as indeed you are doing. For your most worthy presbytery, worthy of God, is so attuned to the bishop as strings to a lyre. Accordingly Jesus Christ is sung by your harmony and symphonic love. 2. Now each of you individually become a chorus, so that in harmony like a symphony, taking your keynote from God, you may sing in unison through Jesus Christ to the Father. The purpose is that he may hear you and recognize through the things that you do well that you are members of his Son. Therefore, it is useful for you to be in blameless unity so that you may always have a share in God.

5.1. For since in a short time I established such fellowship with your bishop, which was not human but spiritual, how much more do I count you blessed who are so united with him as the church is with Jesus Christ and as Jesus Christ is with the Father, so that all things may be harmonious in unity. 2. Let no one be deceived. If one is not within the sanctuary, that person is deprived of the bread of God. For if the prayer of one or two has such force, how much more does that of the bishop and the whole church. 3. Therefore, whoever does not come together in the assembly is already arrogant and has separated himself. For it is written, "God resists the arrogant."[1] Let us, therefore, give diligence not to resist the bishop, in order that we may be submissive to God.

6.1.[2] Now as often as anyone sees the bishop being silent, let that person fear him all the more, for we must receive everyone whom the master sends to his own household just as the one sending him. It is evident, therefore, that we must look to the bishop as to the Lord himself. 6.2. Onesimus himself, therefore, praises highly your orderliness in God, for you all live according to truth and no heresy resides among you. On the contrary, you don't even listen to anyone unless he speaks in truth about Jesus Christ.

Smyrnaeans 7–9

7.1.[3] The heretics stay away from the Eucharist and prayer because they do not confess that the Eucharist is the flesh of our Savior Jesus Christ, which suffered for our sins and which the Father raised up in his kindness. Those who deny the free gift of God, therefore, die in disputes. It would be better for them to love so that they may share in the resurrection. 7.2. It is good to stay away from such persons and not even to talk about them either in private or in public, but to pay attention to the prophets and especially to the Gospel, in which the passion has been manifested to us and the resurrection has been completed. But flee divisions as the worst of evils.

1. Prov 3:34; 1 Pet 5:5.
2. The translation in the following section is from E. Glenn Hinson, ed. and trans., *Understandings of the Church* (Philadelphia: Fortress Press, 1986), 25–26.
3. Ibid., 26–27.

8.1. Flee divisions as the beginning of evils. All of you follow the bishop, as Jesus Christ did the Father, and follow the presbytery as if the apostles. Respect the deacons as the commandment of God. Let no one do anything pertaining to the church apart from the bishop. That Eucharist is to be considered valid which is under the bishop or whomever he should entrust it. 2. Wherever the bishop appears, let the congregation be there, even as wherever Christ Jesus may be, there is the universal church. It is not permitted either to baptize or to hold a love feast apart from the bishop. But whatever the bishop approves is also well pleasing to God, in order everything you do may be secure and valid.

9.1.[4] Finally, it is good that we be serious since we still have time to repent toward God. It is good to know God and a person who honors the bishop has been honored by God. One who does anything without the bishop's knowledge serves the devil.

4. Ibid., 27.

5

Hermas, *Shepherd*

Hermas was a prophet in Rome in the first half of the second century. His *Visions*, *Commandments* (or *Mandates*), and *Parables* (or *Similitudes*) were written over a period of several years. The first selection is from a vision of an elderly woman, who showed Hermas a large tower. Both the woman[1] and the tower[2] were manifestations of the church. The tower was built on water, because one entered the church through baptism. The water has saving power, not of itself, but by the name of God. The church is composed of those made holy by the Lord.

The second selection is part of a further elaboration on the image of the church as a tower, only now Hermas's conversation is with a shepherd. This passage connects with the former, because a person receives the name of the Son of God in baptism. The Son of God is the rock that represents the

1. *Herm. Vis.* 2.4 [8].1.
2. Ibid., 3.3 [11].3.

tower and also the door to the tower. Hermas seems to equate, or at least make parallel, entering the church and entering the kingdom of God. There is a strong affirmation that only through the Son of God does one enter the kingdom of God; not even the angels enter God's presence without him.

Visions 3.3 [11].3, 5

Visions 3.3 [11].3. "I, the church, am the tower that you see being built. I appeared to you both previously and now. Ask whatever you want to know concerning the tower, and I will reveal it to you, in order that you may rejoice with the saints." 4. I said to her, "Lady, since you once considered me worthy to reveal everything to me, reveal it." And she said to me, "Whatever can be revealed to you will be revealed. Only let your heart be with God, and do not be double-minded about what you see."[3] 5. I asked her, "Why, my lady, was the tower built on the waters?" She replied, "Even as I told you before, you do seek diligently. By seeking, therefore, you find the truth. Hear, then, why the tower was built on the waters. It is because your life was saved and will be saved through water. The tower has been founded on the word of the almighty and glorious Name and is strengthened by the invisible power of the Master."

Parables 9.12 [89].1–8

Parables 9.12 [89].1. I said, "First of all, Sir, explain this to me: Who is the rock and the door?" He said, "This rock and door are the Son of God." "How, Sir," I said, "is the rock old and the door new?" "Hear," he said, "and understand, you foolish

3. Michael W. Holmes, ed., *The Apostolic Fathers: Greek Texts and English Translations*, 3rd ed. (Grand Rapids: Baker Academic, 2007), 475–77.

man. 2. The Son of God is much older than all his creation, so that he was a counselor to the Father in his creation. On account of this, the rock is old." "But the gate," I said, "why is it new, Sir?" 3. "Because," he said, "he was revealed in the last days of the consummation. On account of this, the door is new, in order that those going to be saved through it may enter into the kingdom of God. 4. Did you see," he said, "that the stones which have entered through the door have been placed in the construction of the tower, but those that have not entered were removed again to their own place?" I said, "I saw this, Sir." "Thus," he said, "no one will enter into the kingdom of God unless he takes the name of his Son. 5. For if someone wants to enter into a city and that city is walled all around and has one gate, one cannot enter into that city except through its gate, can he?" I said, "How, sir, could it be otherwise?" "If therefore one cannot enter into the city except through its gate, in the same way also," he said, "a person cannot enter into the kingdom of God except through the name of his Son, who was beloved by him. 6.[4] Did you see," he said, "the multitude that was building the tower?" "I saw them, sir," I said. "Those," he said, "are all glorious angels. By them the Lord is walled about. But the door is the Son of God. He is the one entrance to the Lord. Therefore, no one will gain entrance to him except through his Son. 7. Did you see," he said, "the six men, and the glorious and mighty man in their midst, who walked around the tower and rejected the stones from the building?" "I saw them, sir," I said. 8. "The glorious man," he said, "is the Son of God, and those six are the glorious angels who surround him on his right and on his left. No one of the glorious angels will gain entrance to God without him.

4. Sections of 6–8 also from Holmes, *Apostolic Fathers*, 645.

Whoever does not receive his name will not enter into the kingdom of God."

6

Justin Martyr

Justin Martyr was the foremost literary defender of the Christian faith in the mid-second century. He wrote two *Apologies*, which were addressed to the Roman governing authorities, and a *Dialogue with Trypho* (Trypho was a Jew), setting forth the Christian argument with the Jews, in which he showed the Christian appropriation of the Hebrew Scriptures in their Greek translation. Justin sealed his faith by martyrdom in Rome about 165. He presents the Gentile church as in continuity with Israel but superseding it as the true people of God. Christians have their sins forgiven through the name of God's Son, in whom they were baptized. The church as a whole is a priestly people offering pure sacrifices to God. It is a holy people, chosen and redeemed by God, in fulfillment of the promise to Abraham and of the words of the prophets.

Dialogue with Trypho 116.3

116.3. Even so we,[1] who as one person have believed through the name of Jesus[2] in God the Maker of the whole universe, have been stripped of our filthy garments, that is our sins, through the name of his firstborn Son, and have been inflamed with the fire of the word of his calling, we (I say) are the true high priestly race of God. God himself testifies to this, saying that in every place among the nations we offer pure and well-pleasing sacrifices to him.[3] God does not receive sacrifices from anyone except through his priests.

Dialogue with Trypho 119.3–120

119.3. After that Righteous Man [Jesus] was put to death, we [Christians] flourished as another people, and we sprouted new and thriving sheaves of wheat, as the prophets said: "Many nations shall flee to the Lord in that day to become a people, and they shall dwell in all the earth."[4] We [Christians] are not only a people but also a holy people, as we have already shown: "And they shall call them a holy people, redeemed by the Lord."[5] Wherefore, we are not a contemptible people, nor a tribe of barbarians, nor just any nation as the Carians or the Phrygians,[6] 4. but God chose us [Gentile Christians], and he became manifest to those who did not inquire after him. "Behold, I am God," he says, "to a nation that did not call on my name."[7] For this is that nation that God a long time

1. Christians, like the priest Joshua in Zech 3:1–5.
2. The names Jesus and Joshua are the same in Greek.
3. Mal 1:11.
4. Zech 2:11.
5. Isa 62:12.
6. See Thomas Falls, *Writings of Saint Justin Martyr: First Apology*, Fathers of the Church (Washington, DC: Catholic University of America Press, 1948), 331–32.
7. Isa 65:1.

ago promised to Abraham and declared he would make him a father of many nations,[8] not meaning Arabs or Egyptians or Idumeans, since Israel also became the father of a great people, and Esau as well; and there is now a great number of Ammonites. Noah also was the father of Abraham, and indeed of the whole human race; but others were the forebears of other people. What more, then, did Christ grant to Abraham? That he called him with his own voice through the same calling, telling him to depart from the land in which he was living, and he called us all through that same voice, and we have already departed from the country in which we lived according to the evil standards of other citizens of the earth. With Abraham we will inherit the Holy Land, receiving the inheritance of an unfading eternity, being children of Abraham on account of the same faith. For just as he believed the voice of God and it was "accounted to him for righteousness," so also we have believed the voice of God, which has spoken through the apostles of Christ and again was preached through the prophets, and have renounced all things in the world until we die. He promises to Abraham, therefore, a people of like faith—reverent and righteous and pleasing to the Father, but it is not you, "in whom there is no faith."[9]

120. You see how God promises these same things to both Isaac and Jacob: "And all the nations of the earth will be blessed in your seed."[10] And to Jacob, "And all the tribes of the earth shall be blessed in you and in your seed."[11] He no longer says this to Esau or Reuben or any other, but rather to those from whom the Christ was about to come according to the dispensation that was arranged through the Virgin Mary. But

8. Gen 12:1–3 modified.
9. Deut 32:20.
10. Gen 26:4.
11. Gen 28:14.

if you would consider the blessing of Judah, you would understand what I mean. For the seed is divided from Jacob and comes down through Judah and Phares and Jesse and David. Now this was a sign that some of your people would be children of Abraham, being found also in the portion of Christ, but others are also children of Abraham, since they are as the sand on the seashore, which is impotent and fruitless, being numerous and uncountable, but bearing no fruit at all but only drinking the seawater. A multitude of your people is reproved for this reason, drinking bitter and godless doctrines but spitting out the Word of God. He speaks also, therefore, in a statement relating to Judah: "No prince shall be lacking from Judah or leader from his thighs until what has been decreed for him occurs; and he will be what the people are waiting for."[12] Now it is clear that this was not spoken about Judah but about Christ. For not all of us from all the nations are waiting for Judah, but rather for Jesus, who also led your fathers out of Egypt. For until the coming of Christ the prophecy proclaimed, "Until the one who is appointed comes, he too will be what the people are waiting for." He came, therefore, as I have shown in many ways, and Jesus is expected to come again upon the clouds, he whose name you profane and work to have profaned all over the earth.[13]

12. Gen 49:10.
13. E. Glenn Hinson, ed. and trans., *Understandings of the Church* (Philadelphia: Fortress Press, 1986), 34–35.

7

Irenaeus

Irenaeus was bishop of Lyons during the last two decades of the second century. His two major surviving works are the five books *Against Heresies*, directed against the various schools of thought now generally lumped under the name gnostics, but especially the followers of Valentinus, and *Demonstration* [or *Proof*] *of the Apostolic Preaching*, a catechetical book. Although Irenaeus wrote in Greek, *Against Heresies* survives entire only in a Latin translation (the Greek of some passages is preserved in quotations by later writers) and the *Demonstration* survives in an Armenian translation.

Irenaeus is the first major theologian of the emerging orthodox church as it was defining itself against various groups that departed from the apostolic teaching. The first selection, which is one of the passages for which the Greek is preserved, sets forth Irenaeus's statement of what he calls the "rule of truth"[1] and other authors refer to as the "rule of faith." It sets forth the doctrinal standpoint from which Irenaeus confronted those he considered false teachers, and it is a strong affirmation of the united faith preached by the church. The second selection offers a similar summary of essential Christian teaching but includes the structure of the church along with its basic faith;[2] the quoted passage is preceded by the argument that the heretics were of later date than the bishops to whom the apostles committed the churches and so must not represent the original Christian message. The third selection is a succinct statement of Irenaeus's understanding of the place of the church in God's plan of salvation.

The fourth selection is an important statement of the relation of the Holy Spirit to the church and contains an early use of maternal imagery for the church.

The church at Rome was important to Irenaeus's ecclesiology, but how important and on what grounds depend in part on the interpretation of a much-controverted passage that is the fifth selection. Determining its meaning is complicated by the lack of the original Greek. I offer a fairly literal translation of the Latin with expansions that reflect possible meanings. Various interpretations have been offered and are possible, but the important point seems to be that the faithful everywhere preserve the apostolic tradition and Rome reflects this universal consensus.

The final selection from Irenaeus involves a textual problem. Two late Greek quotations read, "Every righteous king has a priestly rank." This is plausible, because the preceding sentence says, "David was made a special priest by God." The earlier Latin translation, however, reads, "Every righteous

1. Irenaeus, *Against Heresies* 1.9.4. Everett Ferguson, *The Rule of Faith: A Guide* (Eugene, OR: Cascade, 2015).
2. For which compare Irenaeus, *Against Heresies* 4.33.7–8.

person has a priestly rank." It is more likely that later Byzantine writers added "king" than that an early Latin translator omitted "king." The decisive evidence comes from Irenaeus himself. In his next book he says, "In the preceding book, we have shown that all the disciples of the Lord are Levites and priests."[3] In regard to the priesthood, all disciples are like the apostles. Irenaeus thus joins Justin Martyr in affirming that the church is a priestly people.

Against Heresies 1.9.5c–1.10.2a

1.9.5c. The truth preached by the church is firm, and that which has been fabricated by these other teachers is lying discourse. 1.10.1. For the church, although dispersed throughout the whole world, as far as the ends of the earth, received from the apostles and their disciples the faith in one God the Father Almighty, who has made the heaven, the earth, the seas, and all things in them; and in one Christ Jesus the Son of God, who was made flesh for our salvation; and in the Holy Spirit, who has proclaimed through the prophets the plans of God and the comings of Christ, both the birth from the virgin, the passion, the rising from the dead, and the bodily ascension into heaven of the beloved Christ Jesus our Lord, and his coming [again] from heaven in the glory of the Father for the summing up of all things and the raising of all humanity, in order that to Christ Jesus, our Lord, God, Savior, and King, according to the good pleasure of the invisible Father, "every knee should bow, of things in heaven, in earth, and under the earth, and that every tongue should confess"[4] to him, and that he might make a just judgment on all, that he might send

3. 5.34.3.
4. Phil 2:10.

the spiritual hosts of wickedness, the angels who transgressed and went into apostasy, and the impious, unjust, lawless, and blasphemers among human beings into the eternal fire; but might grant incorruptible life and eternal glory to those who are righteous, holy, and keep his commandments, and who persevere in his love either from the beginning or by repentance, and surround them with eternal glory.

1.10.2. As we have said before, the church has received this preaching and this faith. Although she is dispersed throughout the world, the church preserves this faith carefully as if living in one house. Similarly she believes these points as if having one and the same soul and heart. She preaches, teaches, and delivers them harmoniously as if possessing one mouth. For even if the languages of the world are different, yet the force of the tradition is one and the same. . . . No one of the rulers in the churches who is powerful in speech will speak other than these teachings; nor will the one weak in speech diminish the tradition. Since the faith is one and the same, neither will the one able to speak at great length concerning it add to it, nor will the one who speaks few words diminish it.

Against Heresies 5.20.1

5.20.1. The path of those belonging to the church, circumscribing the whole world, indeed holding to the firm tradition from the apostles, and giving us to see that the faith of all is one and the same, since all teach that there is one and the same God the Father, believe in the same dispensation of the incarnation of the Son of God, know the same gift of the Spirit, practice the same precepts, observe the same form of organization with regard to the church, expect the same coming of the Lord, and maintain the same salvation of the whole person, that is of soul and body. Assuredly the preaching of the church is true and firm, in which is shown one and the same way of salvation in the whole world. . . . For the church preaches the truth everywhere, and it is the "seven-branched lampstand,"[5] bearing the light of Christ.

Against Heresies 5 Preface

5 Preface. I have pointed out the truth, the plainly public proclamation of the church, that the prophets truly indeed previously proclaimed (even as we have demonstrated), that Christ moreover brought to perfection, that the apostles certainly passed down, from whom the church receiving this truth alone faithfully guards it throughout the whole world and passes it down to her children.

Against Heresies 3.24.1

3.24.1. For where the church is, there also is the Spirit of God; and where the Spirit of God is, there is the church and every grace. The Spirit moreover is truth. Therefore, whoever does not participate in him is neither nurtured in life from the mother's breasts nor receives the most elegant fountain that flows from the body of Christ. Such persons dig for themselves broken cisterns[6] from earthly channels and drink putrid water from them. They flee from the faith of the church lest they be changed. Indeed they reject the Spirit so as not to be instructed.

5. Rev 1:20.
6. Jer 2:13.

Against Heresies 3.3.2

3.3.2. [Since it would take a long time to list the successions in all the churches,] we indicate that of the church of Rome—very great, most ancient, known by all, founded and organized by the two most glorious apostles Peter and Paul—which possesses the tradition from the apostles and the faith announced to all persons that comes down to us through the successions of bishops. . . . For with[7] this church [Rome] on account of its[8] more potent principality[9] it is necessary that every church should agree,[10] that is, those who from every place are faithful, in which church there is always preserved by these who are from every place the tradition that is from the apostles.

Against Heresies 4.8.3

4.8.3. For all the righteous have a priestly rank. Also all the apostles of the Lord are priests, who inherit here neither houses nor fields but always serve the altar and God.

7. Or "to."
8. Or "the."
9. Of the church or of the city?
10. Or "come together," "resort."

8

Letter of the Churches of Vienne and Lyons

A severe persecution of Christians broke out in 177 CE in the cities of Lugdunum (modern Lyons, France) and Vienne in the Rhone valley. Shortly afterward, the churches sent a letter to fellow believers in the provinces of Asia and Phrygia, from which many of their members had come, recounting the persecution, the apostasy of some Christians, and the heroic resistance of others (notably the slave girl Blandina). The letter is preserved in Eusebius, *Church History* 5.1.3–5.3.3, and will be cited according to the divisions of Eusebius's history. Some who initially denied the faith in the face of the persecution then reconsidered and confessed. They were brought back for reexamination before the governor. The quoted selection is an early description of the church as a mother, who received back her erring children. The maternal imagery was reinforced by a Christian physician named Alexander. By making gestures of birth pangs, he encouraged those who had at first denied and then confessed the faith that their repentance could bring rebirth.[1]

Eusebius, *Church History* 5.1.45–48

5.1.45. Through the endurance of the faithful, the immeasurable mercy of Christ was manifested. For through the living the [spiritually] dead were made alive, and those who testified to their faith extended grace to those who did not. And there was much joy to the virgin mother that those whom she miscarried as dead she was receiving back as alive. 5.1.46. For through them many of those who had denied retraced their steps, were conceived again, were rekindled, and learned to confess, when God, who does not desire the death of the sinner but shows kindness to repentance, removed bitterness. . . . 5.1.48. Those who confessed were added to the rank of the martyrs. Those who never had any trace of faith remained on the outside, . . . but all the rest were added to the church.

1. 5.1.49.

9

Clement of Alexandria

The literary activity of Clement of Alexandria falls within the late second century and earliest third century. He was dead by about 215. Clement of Alexandria was well read in pagan, Jewish, and earlier Christian literature. He addressed the concerns of the current philosophical discussions, including especially ethical questions. Hence, he sought an intellectual presentation of Christian faith while also reflecting on matters relevant to the church and the Christian life.

In our first selection, Clement elaborates on one of his favorite images of the church, that of the children of God through their association with Christ, the firstborn Son of God. The second selection adds to this thought the image of the church as mother, as well as believers being members of the body of Christ.

The third selection makes the striking combination of the church as virgin and mother. Clement seems to have Mary the mother of Jesus in mind with the language of virgin mother, but his reference is to the church. This passage is an early instance of adding the church to the usual trinitarian confession of belief in Father, Son, and Holy Spirit, an addition that occurs later in the Apostles' and Nicene Creeds. It is to be noted that the milk supplied by this mother to her children is not her own teachings but the universal Word. The reference to the physical body of Christ as the nourishment is prompted by the use of John 6:53–54 in the context.

The church, according to the fourth selection, is a temple.[1] It is not a place but a people assembled, as in the meaning of the Greek word for church, *ekklēsia*. The contrast of the people with a place is probably not an early allusion to the use of the word "church" for a building where it met but rather was prompted by the discussion of a temple. As a temple, the church is holy and worthy of God. The individuals who make up the church are also pure and holy, characterized by righteous works.

Our last selection from Clement of Alexandria is preceded by a demonstration that the ministry of Jesus and his apostles including Paul belonged to the first century, but the heresies of Basilides, Valentinus, and Marcion arose in the second century. Clement gives a strong affirmation that this true original church is one, even as God and the Lord are each one. It is made up of those collectively predestined from the foundation of the world and is catholic (in the sense of universal). It would be hard to find a more impressive statement of the significance of the church.

Exhortation to the Greeks 9.82

9.82. Come! Come! O my children. "For if you do not become

1. As in the New Testament—1 Cor 3:16; Eph 2:21.

like little children and be born again,"[2] as Scripture says, you may not receive the Father who truly is, "nor will you ever enter into the kingdom of heaven."[3] For how is the stranger permitted to enter? Only, I think, when one is enrolled and becomes a citizen and receives the Father will that person be "among those of the Father,"[4] be counted worthy to share in the inheritance and participate in the Father's kingdom with his true Son, the "beloved."[5] For this is the firstborn church, composed of many good children. These are "the firstborn ones enrolled in heaven" who celebrate festival with "so many myriads of angels."[6] We too are the firstborn children, the foster children of God, who are the genuine friends of the "Firstborn One,"[7] the first of other human beings who have come to perceive God, the first ones drawn away from sins, the first ones separated from the devil.

Instructor 1.5.21–22

1.5.21. [After quoting Isa 66:12–13] The mother brings the children to herself, and we ourselves seek the mother, the church. That which is weak and altogether tender, which on account of weakness is in need of help, is shown favor, sweetness, and pleasantness, since God does not avoid giving help to such as these.

1.5.22. [Isaac "sporting" with his wife[8] is a type of Christ.] [Christ], having delivered her from death, laughed, sporting and rejoicing with his bride, who is the helper of our salvation,

2. Clement alludes to Matt 18:3 and John 3:5 addressing Christians as children.
3. Matt 18:3.
4. Luke 2:49.
5. Cf. Matt 3:17; Mark 1:11; Luke 3:22; John 1:34. E. Glenn Hinson, ed. and trans., *Understandings of the Church* (Philadelphia: Fortress Press, 1986), 46.
6. Heb 12:22–23.
7. Rom 8:29; Col 1:15, 18.
8. Gen 26:8.

namely the church. To her is given the steadfast name of endurance. This is so, since she alone remains forever, rejoicing always, and stands firm through the endurance of believers, who are members of Christ.

Instructor 1.6.42.1–43.1

1.6.42.1. O mystic marvel! The universal Father is one; one also is the universal Word; and the Holy Spirit is one and the same everywhere; and one only is the virgin mother, whom I love to call church. The mother by herself did not have milk, because she did not become a wife alone. She is at the same time virgin and mother, undefiled as a virgin, loving as a mother. Calling her children, she nurses with holy milk, the Word suitable for children. Therefore, she did not have milk, because the milk was the Word (the fair and proper child), the body of Christ, which nourishes the youth with the word. 2. Accordingly she did not have milk, because the milk was the Word, this good and fair child, the body of Christ, which nourishes the new people which the Lord himself bore with physical pain, which the Lord himself wrapped in his precious blood. 3. O holy birth! O holy swaddling clothes! The Word is everything to the infant, father and mother and instructor and nurse. "Eat my flesh," he says, "and drink my blood."[9] The Lord supplies these suitable foods for us and hands us his flesh and pours out his blood, and nothing is lacking for the children's growth. 43.1. O paradoxical mystery! We are commanded to lay aside the old physical corruption, just like stale food, and, taking a new garment, that of Christ, to take him up if possible to receive him within ourselves and place the Savior in our hearts, so that we may annul the lusts of our flesh.[10]

9. See John 6:53.

Miscellanies 7.5.29

7.5.29. If the sacred is understood in a twofold way, both God himself and the building in his honor, how then is the church which is through knowledge for the honor of God not properly holy? Would we not call holy what is much more worthy of God and is not constructed by handicraft skill nor embellished by what is acquired by begging but made into a temple by the will of God? For I do not now call the place the church but the gathering of the elect. This temple is better for the reception of the greatness worthy of God. . . . Here too [in the true gnostic] we would find the representation, the divine and holy image, in the righteous soul, whenever this soul attains blessedness, seeing that it has been purified and performs blessed deeds.

Miscellanies 7.17.107

7.17.107. From what has been said, therefore, it is evident, I think, that the true church which is truly from the beginning is one. Into it are enrolled those who are intentionally righteous. Since God is one, and the Lord is one, accordingly that which is in the highest degree honorable is praised for its oneness, being an imitation of the one First Principle. Therefore, joined with the nature of the One is the one church, which heresies attempt to cut into many. Hence, in substance, in thought, in origin, and in preeminence we say the original and universal church stands alone. It brings together into the "unity of the one faith,"[11] that is of the individual covenants (or rather of the one covenant differing in various times) by the will of the one God through the one Lord, those already appointed, whom God before the foundation of the world knew that they would

10. Hinson, *Understandings of the Church*, 48–49.
11. Eph 4:13.

be righteous and foreordained them. Yet the preeminence of the church, even as the principle of union, is in its oneness surpassing all other things and having nothing like or equal to itself.

10

Tertullian

Tertullian was a rhetorician in Carthage, North Africa. His life spanned approximately 160 to 220. He was a rigorist in moral matters and so often at odds with the leadership of the churches. Nevertheless, he was a learned and effective defender of the faith and had a formative influence on the development of Latin Christian theology. His rigorism gave him sympathy with the Montanist (or "new prophecy") movement, but it is not certain that he ever formally separated from the great church, although he continued to be critical of certain practices contrary to the Montanist emphases.

Justin Martyr wrote an account of a regular Sunday assembly of the church.[1] Tertullian in addition to describing an assembly recorded an account of an *agapē* (love feast). Both apologists sought to disabuse Roman authorities of the popular slanders that the Christian gatherings were occasions of immorality.

1. Justin Martyr, *1 Apology* 67.

Tertullian's account is included here not only for its description of an assembly and a love feast but especially for what it tells about the nature of the church, its discipline, and the role of elders. Tertullian's treatise *On Repentance* gives more details on the administration of discipline for serious sins, a procedure presided over by the elders of the congregation. In seeking to overcome the hesitancy to submit to the humiliating practice, Tertullian affirms that the church is Christ, as his body, and so takes no pleasure in the punishment of its members.

Tertullian in his later writings wanted to curtail sharply the readmission of erring Christians to the church. In his treatise *On Modesty*, where he identifies himself with the "new prophecy" by the Paraclete in the Montanist movement, he discusses the power of the church to forgive postbaptismal sins. Tertullian understood the parables of the lost sheep and of the lost coin in Luke 15 as referring to saving pagans and not the restoration of lost members of the church. His quotation by those who interpreted them as referring to fallen church members[2] is included here to point to the image of the church as a flock under the Good Shepherd, Christ. Tertullian grants the right of the church to readmit the fallen to fellowship, but he says that according to the Paraclete it will not exercise this power to avoid encouraging others to sin. He then makes the claim that it is the church of the Spirit, not the church of bishops, that possesses this power.[3]

Against followers of Marcion and the various gnostic teachers, Tertullian championed the one church derived from the apostles and following their teaching. A church was apostolic if it traced its origin back to apostles or to churches

2. Tertullian, *On Modesty* 7.4.
3. Ibid., 21.16–17.

founded by apostles and held to the same doctrine taught by the apostles. The church at Rome was an example of the churches founded by apostles, especially distinguished by the martyrdoms of Peter and Paul.[4] These churches followed the same faith and practice. Their disciplined organization contrasted with the disorder in heretical churches. Tertullian's (exaggerated?) negative description of heretical groups shows what was valued in the order of catholic churches. The heretics did not maintain the distinctions that had become standardized in orthodox churches. In *On Prescription against Heretics* 41.8, Tertullian implicitly denies priestly duties to the laity, but in his later *Exhortation to Chastity* 7, he affirms the view of earlier writers that all laymen are priests.

Among the images of the church, Tertullian in writing against the Jews gives prominence to the church as God's temple. Christ is "the true temple of God,"[5] but in the same chapter the church is said to be "God's temple."[6] In the same context, Tertullian affirms the priestly nature of the church.[7]

A favorite image of the church for Tertullian, as it continued to be for Latin Christianity, was that of mother. In addition to the passage quoted from *On the Soul* 43.10, where he draws the parallels between Adam and Christ and Eve and the church (both the mother of the living), note *On Prayer* 2, "Our mother the church," and *To the Martyrs* 1, "the provision which our mother the church makes from her bountiful breasts," and *On Monogamy* 7, where the one God the Father is paired with "our mother the church."

4. Tertullian, *On Prescription against Heretics* 36.4.
5. Tertullian, *Against the Jews* 13.15.
6. Ibid., 13.25.
7. Ibid., 14.9.

Apology 39

39.1. I will proceed then to explain the features of this Christian sect not so much to refute the evil as to show the good, and perhaps also to disclose the truth.[8]

39.2. We are a body with a common feeling of religion, a unity of discipline, and a covenant of hope. We meet together in an assembly and congregation so that praying to God we may win him over by the strength of our prayers. This kind of force is pleasing to God. We pray also for emperors, for their servants and those in authority, for the order of the world, for peaceful circumstances, for the delay of the end. 39.3. We meet together in order to read the sacred texts, if the nature of the times compels us to warn about or recognize anything present. In any case, with the holy words we feed our faith, we arouse our hope, we confirm our confidence. We strengthen the instruction of the precepts no less by inculcations; in the same place, there are also exhortations, rebukes, and divine censure. 39.4. For judgment is administered with great authority, as among those in the presence of God, and it is the supreme anticipation of the judgment to come if any has so sinned that this person is banished from participation in our prayer, our gatherings, and all holy fellowship. Elders who are proved men preside over us, having attained that honor not by purchase but by recognition. For not anything of God's is determined by purchase. 39.5. Although we have a kind of money chest, it is not gathered from the fees of our leaders as if religion were a matter of purchase. Every individual puts in a small contribution on the monthly day, or when he wishes and only if he wishes and is able. For no one is compelled, but each

8. E. Glenn Hinson, ed. and trans., *Understandings of the Church* (Philadelphia: Fortress Press, 1986), 52.

contributes voluntarily. These contributions are trust funds of piety. 6. These donations are, as it were, "deposits of piety." The money is not spent, you can be sure, on sumptuous foods or drinking bouts or fancy restaurants, but to bury poor people and to meet the needs of boys and girls and destitute parents, and also old people now forced into idleness at homes, and likewise those who have suffered shipwreck, and if any in the mines and on the islands and in prisons become wards of their confession insofar as it is for the sake of the church.

7. But the work of this kind of love especially brands us in the eyes of some. "Look," they say, "how they love one another," for they hate one another, "and how they are prepared to die for each other," for they are more prepared to kill each other. 8. But they also get angry at us because we think of one another as brothers and sisters, for no other reason, I think, than because among them every affectionate family name is feigned. But we are also your brothers and sisters by virtue of having one mother nature, although you are hardly human because evil brothers and sisters. 9. How much more worthy are those to be called and regarded as brothers and sisters who have known one Father, God, who have imbibed of the one Spirit of holiness, who have struggled from the one womb of the same ignorance to the one light of truth? 10. But perhaps we are thought to be less legitimate because no tragedy cries out from our fraternity or because we remain brothers and sisters despite those family possessions that destroy fraternity among you. 11. And so we who are related in mind and soul do not hesitate to share our things. We share everything except wives. 12. We give up our commonality in the only place where other persons practice commonality. They not only take possession of the wives of their friends but also very tolerantly lend theirs to their friends, following, I think, the example

of the greater and wiser of them, the Greek Socrates and the Roman Cato, who shared with friends their wives, whom they married to bear children not only for themselves but also for others. 13. I don't know whether that was against their will or not, for why should they worry about chastity when their husbands gave it away so readily? What model of Attic wisdom! What a model of Roman seriousness! The philosopher and magistrate are pimps!

14. Is it any wonder, then, that such love as Christians have is ridiculed? For you pummel even our little suppers not only as wasteful but also as infamously wicked. "The Megarians feast like they were about to die tomorrow; but they build like they were never going to die!" 15. But one sees the speck in another person's eye more easily than the log in one's own. The air is polluted with the belches of so many tribes and curias and decurias. The Salii will have to borrow money to hold their banquets. Accountants will have to tell you the costs of the Herculanean tithes and sumptuous banquets. The best of chefs is selected for the Apaturian, Dionysian, and Attic mysteries. Firemen will be called out to put out the flames of the Serapian banquet. Yet a hullaballoo is raised only about the supper room of Christians![9]

39.16. Our feast shows its motive by its name. It is called by the Greek word *agapē*, love. Whatever is reckoned the cost, money spent in the name of piety is gain, since with that refreshment we benefit the needy. It is not, as among you, a case where parasites aspire to the glory of servile freedom and under control of the belly stuff themselves beyond abuse,[10] as is so with God, there is a greater consideration for the lowly. 39.17. If the reason for our common meal is honorable,

9. Ibid., 53–54.
10. See Hinson, *Understandings of the Church*, 54.

appraise the subsequent order of procedure by its purpose. Since it is a religious duty, it permits nothing vile, nothing immodest. We do not recline at the table before prayer to God is first tasted. 39.18. We eat the amount that satisfies the hungry; we drink as much as is beneficial to the modest. We satisfy ourselves as those who remember that even during the night we must worship God; we converse as those who know that the Lord listens. After the washing of hands and lighting of lamps, each one who is able is called into the center to chant praise to God either from the holy Scriptures or from his own talents. This is a proof of how much is drunk. Prayer in like manner concludes the meal. 39.19. We depart from it not as crowds of killers or bands of vagabonds nor to get involved in lascivious acts, but rather to exercise the same care for modesty and chastity as those who gathered not so much for supper as for instruction.

39.20. This gathering of Christians must be condemned very deservedly as illicit if it is like those that are illicit. It must be condemned very deservedly if it is not unlike those that are condemned, if anyone lays against it a valid complaint such as is laid against secret factions. 39.21. When did we ever gather for some pernicious purpose? Assembled we are what we are when dispersed, together what we are as individuals, injuring nobody, troubling nobody. When the righteous, when the good assemble; when the pious, when the pure gather, it must not be called faction but a curia.[11]

On Repentance 9.2–5; 10.4–6

9.2. This act [second repentance, for sins committed after baptism], which is most often expressed by the Greek term,

11. Hinson, *Understandings of the Church*, 54–55.

is *exomologēsis*, by which we confess our transgressions to the Lord. Not that he is ignorant of them, but inasmuch as by confession satisfaction is arranged, from confession repentance is born, by repentance God is appeased. 9.3. Thus *exomologēsis* is a discipline for human abasement and humiliation, enjoining that behavior which brings mercy. 9.4. It commands with regard to the very clothes and dress to lie in sackcloth and ashes, to cover the body with soiled clothing, to lay the soul low with lamentations, to exchange severe treatment for those sins that were committed; for the rest to allow only plain food and drink, not (to be sure) for the stomach's sake but the soul's. And for the most part it commands indeed to strengthen prayers with fasting, to heave sighs, to weep, to groan day and night to your Lord God, to fall prostrate before the elders, to kneel before God's dear ones, to enjoin on all the brothers and sisters to be ambassadors on behalf of your supplications. 9.5. All these things *exomologēsis* performs so that it may make repentance acceptable, so that it may honor God by the fear of danger, so that by itself pronouncing judgment on the sinner may act in place of God's wrath and by temporal afflictions may (I do not say frustrate but) expunge eternal punishments. . . .

10.4. Among brothers and fellow slaves, where there is a common hope, fear, joy, distress, suffering, because of a common Spirit from a common Lord and Father, why do you think these brothers to be other than yourself? 10.5. . . . The body cannot feel gladness at the suffering of one of its members; it is necessary that it grieve as a whole and labor together for a remedy. 10.6. With one or two is the church, and the church is Christ. Therefore, when you prostrate yourself at the brothers' knees, you are handling Christ, you are entreating Christ. Likewise, when they shed tears over you, Christ is suffering, Christ is supplicating the Father.

On Modesty 7.4; 21.16–17

7.4. [Tertullian quotes the understanding by the majority in his church concerning Luke 15:3–7.] "'Sheep' properly is a Christian, and 'flock' is the people of the Lord's church, and Christ is the 'Good Shepherd.'[12] Hence, by 'sheep' one must understand a Christian who has strayed from the flock of the church."

21.16. Now the church itself, properly and principally, is the Spirit himself, in whom is the Trinity of one divinity—Father, Son, and Holy Spirit. He gathers that church which the Lord states to be in "three."[13] 21.17. Accordingly from that time forward, whatever the number of all who agree in this faith are accounted by its Author and Initiator a church. For this reason the church certainly excuses faults, but it is the church of the Spirit through a spiritual man, not the church of a number of bishops. For the right and power of judging are the Lord's, not the servant's; belong to God himself, not to the priest.

On Prescription against Heretics 20

20.1. Christ Jesus, our Lord (if I may speak in this way for a little while), whoever he is, Son of whatever God, man and God of whatever substance, teacher of whatever faith, promisor of whatever mercy, 2. while he lived on earth, declared what he was, what he had been, what the Father's will was that he was serving, what was decreed that human beings must do. He declared this either openly to the people or privately to his

12. John 10:11.
13. Matt 18:20.

disciples, from whom he chose twelve as the chief ones at his side and designated them as teachers of the nations.[14] 3. And so when one of them was excised as he was departing to the Father after the resurrection, he ordered the other eleven to go and teach the nations, baptizing into the Father and the Son and the Holy Spirit.[15]

20.4. [The twelve apostles] went out to the world and proclaimed the same doctrine and same faith to the nations. 20.5. Similarly in each city they founded churches, from whom subsequently other churches have borrowed and are daily borrowing the seeds of doctrine in order to become churches. 20.6. In this way indeed they are themselves considered as apostolic in that they are the offspring of apostolic churches. 20.7. Everything must necessarily be appraised according to its origin. For this reason, so many and so great churches are yet the one apostolic church from which all are derived. 20.8. Since all are primitive and all are apostolic, so all are one. The sharing of peace, the name of brotherhood, the common bond of hospitality prove their unity. 20.9. These privileges no other system directs than the one tradition of this very mystery.

On Prescription against Heretics 32

32.1. But if any heresies dare to plant themselves in the apostolic age so that they may appear to have been handed down by the apostles because they were under apostles, we can say,[16] "Show the origins of your churches; roll out the order of your bishops, in what manner extending down by succession from the beginning so that the first bishop had his source and predecessor someone from the apostles or an apostolic man

14. Mark 4:34.
15. Matt 28:19. Hinson, *Understandings of the Church*, 57.
16. Ibid.

and who moreover remained with the apostles." 2. For this is how the apostolic churches transmit their lists. The church of Smyrna, for instance, records that Polycarp was called by John, and the church of Rome records that Clement was ordained by Peter. 3. In the same manner, the other churches put forward those appointed to the episcopate by the apostles, who transmitted the apostolic seed to them. 4. Let the heretics pretend they have anything like that. For what is unlawful for them after blasphemy?[17] 32.5. Their very doctrine, compared with the apostolic doctrine, is declared by its own diversity and contradictions to have for its author neither any one of the apostles nor any apostolic man. The apostles would not have taught contradictory things among themselves, nor would apostolic men who were taught by the apostles have prescribed those things contrary to the apostles. 32.6. Those churches that are being established daily are considered no less apostolic by reason of the kinship in doctrine since they agree together in the same faith. 32.7. Then let all the heresies when summoned by our churches to the double standard [succession from the apostles and agreement with apostolic doctrine] prove in what way they consider themselves to be apostolic. 8. But of course they are not, and cannot prove they are what they are not. They are not accepted in peace and communion by churches that are in any way apostolic, of course, because they are in no way apostolic on account of the diversity of their creed.[18]

On Prescription against Heretics 36

36.1. Move through the apostolic churches in which the very

17. Ibid.
18. Ibid., 57–58.

chairs of the apostles preside in their places, in which their authentic writings are read, sounding the voice and representing the appearance of each of them individually. 36.2. If Achaia is nearest to you, you have Corinth. If you are not far from Macedonia, you have Philippi. If you can travel to Asia, you have Ephesus. But if you are close to Italy, you have Rome, from which authority has come to us also. 36.3. How fortunate is this church, for which the apostles poured out all their teaching with their blood! Where Peter attained to a death like the Lord's, where Paul was crowned with John's death, from where the apostle John, after he suffered no harm from immersion in boiling oil, was sent into exile on an island! 36.4. Let us see what she learned, what she taught, since she has established friendship with the African churches also. 36.5. [The church at Rome] knows one Lord God, Creator of the universe; and Jesus Christ Son of God the Creator [born] from the Virgin Mary; and the resurrection of the flesh. She unites the Law and Prophets with the Gospels and apostolic writings, from which she drinks her faith. This faith she seals with water [baptism], clothes with the Holy Spirit, nourishes with the Eucharist, is exhorted to martyrdom; and this faith receives no one who opposes this doctrine. 6. This is the teaching I no longer need tell, which was predicting future heresies but from which heresies would go forth. But they are not from it because they came into existence against it. 36.7. Even the rough wild olive arises necessarily from the core of the tame and rich olive; even the empty and useless fig comes out of the seed of the best and sweetest fig. 36.8. In the same way, heresies too come from our tree, although not of our type, having a grain of truth but actually forests of lies.[19]

19. Ibid., 58.

On Prescription against Heretics 41

41.1. Also, I should not omit a description of the behavior of the heretics—how futile, how worldly, how merely human it is, without dignity, without authority, without discipline—that is consistent with their faith. 41.2. To begin with, it is uncertain who is a catechumen and who is one of the faithful; they all enter together, they hear together, they pray together. Even if gentiles gather with them, they will "cast what is holy to the dogs" and "pearls [although not real pearls] before swine."[20] 41.3. They strive for simplicity by abandonment of discipline, care for which on our part they call "pandering." They also are in communion with everybody everywhere. 41.4. For it doesn't matter to them how diverse their views are, so long as they agree to battle against the one truth. All are inflated. All offer knowledge. Catechumens are "perfect" before they have been instructed.[21] 41.5. The women among the heretics—how undisciplined they are. They dare to teach, to dispute, to perform exorcisms, to promise healings, perhaps even to baptize. 41.6. Their ordinations are random, lack seriousness, are unstable. They put in office neophytes, those entangled with secular affairs, those who apostatize from us in order to capture them by flattery because they cannot do so by truth. 41.7. Nowhere is it easier to advance than in the camp of the rebels where it is meritorious merely to be there.[22] 41.8. Thus today one man is their bishop, tomorrow another; today one man is a deacon who tomorrow is a reader; today one is a presbyter who tomorrow is a layman. Indeed, they bestow on laymen priestly duties.

20. Matt 7:6.
21. Hinson, *Understandings of the Church*, 58–59.
22. Ibid., 59.

Exhortation to Chastity 7

7. Are not we who are laymen also priests? The Scripture says, "He made us a kingdom and priests to his God and Father."[23] The authority of the churches and the honor sanctified by the gathering of the order established the difference between the order and the people. What is more, where there is no gathering of the ecclesiastical order, you both offer [the Eucharist] and baptize, yourself alone a priest. But also where there are three,[24] there is a church, although they are laymen.

Against the Jews 13.25; 14.9

13.25. The Lord of hosts took away from the Jews and from Jerusalem[25] among other things "the wise architect" [Christ], who builds the church, the temple of God, and the holy city and the house of the Lord.

14.9. After the expiation of all sins, the priests of the spiritual temple, that is of the church, enjoy something of a sacrificial feast of the Lord's grace.

On the Soul 43.10

43.10. For if Adam was a figure of Christ, Adam's sleep was the death of Christ, who slept in death so that from the wound on his side similarly is figured the church, the true mother of the living.

23. Rev 1:6.
24. Matt 18:20.
25. Isa 3:1.

11

Hippolytus

Hippolytus of Rome was active in the first third of the third century. Several important works are attributed to him, including a *Commentary on Daniel*, the *Apostolic Tradition*, and *Refutation of All Heresies*. Some scholars assign the body of writings attributed to him to two or three writers or to a school associated with him. *On Christ and Antichrist* reflects an interest in eschatological themes, but the selection chosen for quotation gives an imaginative comparison of the church facing the perils of the world to a ship on a restless sea. Justin Martyr had earlier seen the mast of a ship as among the images in nature of the cross.[1]

On Christ and Antichrist 59

59. [Commenting on Isa 18:1-2:] We who hope in the Son of

1. Justin Martyr, *1 Apology* 55.

God are persecuted and trodden down by unbelievers. For the "wings of the ships"[2] are the churches. The "sea" is the world, in which the church like a ship is tempest-tossed in the open sea but is not destroyed, for she has with herself the experienced Pilot, Christ. She bears in her middle also the trophy which marks death, as bearing with herself the cross of the Lord. Her prow is the east; her stern is the west; her hold is the south; and the tillers are the two Testaments. The ropes stretched around her are the love of Christ, which holds together the church. The fishing net that she carries with her is the "laver of regeneration,"[3] which renews believers and where these things are made clear. There is present like wind from heaven the Spirit, by which believers are sealed for God. Iron anchors always accompany her, the holy commandments of Christ himself, which are strong as iron. She has sailors on the right and on the left, holy angels as attendants through whom the church is always supported and guarded. Her ladder leading up to the sail yard is an image of the sign of the passion of Christ that draws the faithful upward to heaven. The mastheads[4] at the peak raised to the height are the company of prophets, martyrs, and apostles who are at rest in the kingdom of Christ.

2. Isa 18:1, Greek.
3. Titus 3:5.
4. Meaning is uncertain.

12

Pseudo-Clement

The core of the Pseudo-Clementine literature belongs to the third century but incorporates some material from the second century and was extensively redacted in the fourth century. The excerpt quoted here is from the *Letter to James*, supposedly from Clement of Rome to James of Jerusalem. I place it here because, like the preceding selection from Hippolytus, *On Christ and Antichrist* 59, it describes the church under the image of a ship. The points of comparison, however, are quite different. The only common elements are likening the sea to the world with its persecutions and temptations, Christ as the pilot of the ship, and the destination of the ship as the kingdom of God.

Letter to James 14

14. The whole reality of the church is like to a large ship carrying through a violent storm persons who although from many places yet desire to live in the one city of the good

kingdom. Therefore, let God be for you the Master of the ship. And let the Pilot be compared to Christ, the officer at the bow[1] to the bishop, the sailors to the presbyters, the boatswains to the deacons, the ship's stewards to the catechists. Let the multitude of the brothers and sisters be compared to the passengers, the world to the deep sea, the contrary winds to temptations. The persecutions, dangers, and all manner of afflictions are like mighty waves; the winds of winter storms blowing from the land are like the speeches of deceivers and false prophets; rugged promontories and jagged rocks are like judges in authority who threaten terrible things; the convergence of two currents and places full of wild beasts are like persons who are unreasonable and cast doubts on the promises of truth. Let the hypocrites be considered as comparable to pirates. Moreover, think of a strong whirlpool, Charybdis of Tartarus, murderous shipwrecks, and deadly breaking apart of ships to be nothing other than sins. In order, therefore, that you may sail with a fair wind and be carried without danger into the harbor of the hoped-for city, pray so as to be heard. Prayers are heard when accompanied with good deeds.

1. Or chief oarsman.

13

Origen

Origen lived approximately from 185 to 251. He was a teacher in Alexandria but ran afoul of the bishop Demetrius and moved to Caesarea in Palestine, where he was ordained a presbyter. Origen was the greatest intellect of the ancient church. His prodigious memory made him a walking concordance of the Bible. Although suspected of heretical teaching, he was a devoted churchman and dedicated student of the Bible. He is especially remembered for his nonliteral moral and spiritual interpretation of the Scriptures, set forth in many homilies and commentaries.

Celsus was a pagan philosopher who in the last quarter of the second century wrote *The True Word*, an attack on Christianity. Origen's response, *Against Celsus*, was the major Greek apologetic writing from the early church. One of Celsus's charges against Christians was that they invited only "sinners," in contrast to Hellenistic cults that invited only the "worthy" into their membership and sanctuaries.[1] Origen acknowledged that Christians invited all, including sinners, but in order to make them better. The church is made up of converted sinners. In affirming the changes effected by Christian teaching, Origen makes one of his statements on the notable growth of the church by his day.[2]

Origen contrasted the good order in the churches with the disorder in the civic councils and assemblies of the Hellenistic cities that he knew.[3] He repeated Clement of Alexandria's point about the church not being a literal building[4] but a building made of faith, wisdom, and love. The twin essentials of those who are members of the church are a good life and correct faith. Origen picked up the image of the church as the body of Christ to make a comparison of the Word in the church to a soul in the body. In the context, this comparison is used to make an argument for the union of the person of Jesus with the divine Word.[5] In his *Commentary on John*, Origen deals extensively with John's account of Jesus' cleansing the temple in John 2. He particularly comments on the combination of the body of Christ and the temple as images of the church. Different systems of numbering are applied to this commentary; I have employed that by Ronald Heine in his translation in the Fathers of the Church series.

Origen's *Commentary on the Song of Songs* gave opportunity for extensive development of the theme of the church as bride of Christ. This includes the imagery of the church as mother, for the Word through the church begets children. Origen typically uses the imagery of bride individually for the soul and

1. Origen, *Against Celsus* 3.49–59.
2. Ibid., 1.67.
3. Ibid., 3.29–30.
4. Origen, *Commentary on the Song of Songs* 3.13.
5. Origen, *Against Celsus* 6.48.

collectively for the church. The passage in *Commentary on the Song of Songs* 1.1 contains the important definition of the church as "the whole assembly of saints." The image of church as bride led naturally to the image of the church as mother, a description current among Greeks as well as Latins. According to Origen, God the Father claims the church as his wife, and through her, the mother church, he produces children.[6] Origen applied the words of Matt 16:18 to everyone who makes the confession Peter made in 16:16, so every true believer becomes a rock and a Peter.

Against Celsus 1.67

1.67. We say, therefore, that the whole inhabited world of human beings contains the work of Jesus, for in it reside the churches of God, which through Jesus have changed from so many myriads of evils. Indeed the name of Jesus still removes terrifying distractions from the minds of human beings as well as demons and illnesses. It produces a marvelous gentleness and moderation of character, benevolence, kindness, and mildness in those who not hypocritically for livelihood or some human needs but those who genuinely receive the word about God, Christ, and the coming judgment.

Against Celsus 3.29–30

3.29. The assemblies[7] of God that have been instructed in Christ when they are compared with the assemblies[8] of the citizens in the cities where they are located are "as lights in the world."[9] For who would not acknowledge that even those "inferior"

6. *On Proverbs* 17.21.
7. Churches—*ekklēsiai.*
8. *Ekklēsiais.*
9. Phil 2:15.

in the churches and of less account in comparison with the better sort are a great deal better than the assemblies in those districts?

3.30. For the assembly[10] of God in Athens is meek and stable, wishing to please the God who is over all, but the assembly of the Athenians is seditious and in no way comparable to the assembly of God. And you will say the same concerning the assembly of God that is in Corinth and the assembly of the citizens of Corinth [and also in Alexandria]. . . . In the same way, you would find also the council of the assembly of God when compared to the [civic] council in that city. Any council members of the church, if there is a city of God in the place, are worthy to take part in the government in that city, but the council members everywhere are not worthy of the appointed authority that they appear to exercise over the citizens.

Commentary on the Song of Songs 3.13

3.13 [on Song of Songs 2:9–13]. But the soul, which is said to be "in the Church," is understood not as being situated within the buildings which the walls enclose, but rather as being placed within the bulwarks of faith and the edifice of wisdom, and covered over with the lofty gables of charity. What makes a soul to be in the house of the Church is, therefore, good conduct and belief in right doctrines.[11]

Against Celsus 6.48

6.48. We say that the divine words declare that the body of Christ animated by the Son of God is the whole church of God

10. Church.
11. R. P. Lawson, trans., *Origen: The Song of Songs: Commentary and Homilies*, Ancient Christian Writers 26 (Westminster, MD: Newman Press, 1957), 232.

and the members of this body as a whole are those who are believers. Since as a soul gives life and moves the body, which has not by itself the natural ability of motion like a living being, even so the Word, moving and activating the whole body to the necessary things, moves the church and each member of the church, so that they do nothing apart from the Word.

Commentary on John 10.16.133–34

10.16.133. Jesus found in the temple,[12] which is also said to be the house of the Savior's Father,[13] that is in the church or in the proclamation of the healthful word of the church, some who were making the house of the Father a house of commerce. 10.16.134. And Jesus always finds some such in the temple. For when in what is named the church, which is the house "of the living God, the pillar and support of the truth,"[14] are there not some money changers?

Commentary on John 10.20.228–29

10.20.228. Both indeed, the temple and the body of Jesus, according to one interpretation, appear to me to be a type of the church inasmuch as it is called a "temple"[15] built of "living stones," being a spiritual house "for a holy priesthood,"[16] built "upon the foundation of the apostles and prophets, Christ Jesus being the chief cornerstone."[17] 10.20.229. Through the statement, "You are the body of Christ and individually members,"[18] [we know that] even if the union of the stones of

12. John 2:12.
13. John 2:16.
14. 1 Tim 3:15.
15. Eph 2:21.
16. 1 Pet 2:5.
17. Eph 2:20.
18. 1 Cor 12:27.

the temple seem to be broken, or all the bones of Christ be "scattered," as is written in the twenty-first Psalm,[19] by the plots in persecutions and afflictions of those who wage war on the unity of the temple with persecutions, the temple and the body will be raised on the third day.

Commentary on John 10.23.263–64

10.23.263. If the body of Jesus is said to be his temple,[20] it is worth inquiring whether this must be understood in a singular sense or each of the things written concerning the temple must be distinguished with regard to the saying concerning the body of Jesus, either the body he received from the virgin or the church, which is said to be his body,[21] even as we are named members of his body by the apostle.[22] 10.20.264. . . . The body understood either way is to be called a temple, since even as the temple [in Jerusalem] had the glory of God dwelling in it, so the Firstborn of all creation[23] possessing the image and glory of God[24] is properly said to be the temple bearing the image of God, whether with respect to his body or to the church.

Commentary on the Song of Songs, Prologue 2

Prologue 2. The Scripture before us [the Song of Songs], therefore, speaks of this love with which the blessed soul is kindled and inflamed towards the Word of God; it sings by the Spirit the song of the marriage whereby the Church is joined and allied to Christ the heavenly Bridegroom, desiring to be united to Him through the Word, so that she may conceive by

19. Ps 21:15, Greek.
20. John 2:21.
21. Eph 1:22–23.
22. Eph 5:30.
23. Col 1:15.
24. John 1:14.

Him and be saved through this chaste begetting of children, when they—conceived as they are indeed of the seed of the Word of God, and born and brought forth by the spotless Church, or by the soul that seeks nothing bodily, nothing material, but is aflame with the single love of the Word of God—shall have persevered in faith and holiness with sobriety.[25]

Commentary on the Song of Songs 1.1

1.1 [on Song of Songs 1:2a]. The spiritual interpretation too is equally in line with that which we pointed out in our prologue; the appellations of Bride and Bridegroom denote either the Church in her relation to Christ, or the soul in her union with the Word of God. . . . But let us see if the inner meaning also can be fittingly supplied along these lines. Let it be the Church who longs for union with Christ; but the Church, you must observe, is the whole assembly of the saints. So it must be the Church as a corporate personality who speaks and says, "I am sated with the gifts which I received as betrothal presents or as dowry before my marriage."[26]

On Proverbs 17.21

17.21. A prudent son gives joy to his mother, the benevolence of God. She introduces us to the God and Father himself, as sons who have been weaned and allowed solid food. The result is that as his Son, Jesus Christ, who became a brother in likeness to us, so we also might live as free citizens in deed and word. Our mother is the church, whom the God and Father by the Holy Spirit betrothed to himself as a wife, for he always begets

25. Lawson, *Origen: The Song of Songs*, 38–39.
26. Ibid., 58–59.

through her for himself sons and daughters. Our Father God and the mother, the church, are made glad with regard to those instructed in the knowledge and wisdom of God, but in regard to those uninstructed they are always distressed and grieved, when we do not want to turn and be saved but want to remain in wickedness.

Commentary on Matthew 12.11

12.11. But if you think the whole church was built by God upon that one Peter alone, what would you say concerning John, "the son thunder,"[27] or each one of the apostles? Truly, therefore, shall we dare to say that "the gates of Hades shall not prevail"[28] against Peter only but will prevail against the rest of the apostles and the perfect? . . . If "I will give to you the keys of the kingdom of heaven"[29] are common to the others also, how are not also conferred on them all the things said in the passage as spoken to Peter. . . . What the letter of the Gospel says to that Peter, so its spirit teaches to everyone who becomes what Peter was. For all bear the name "rock" who are imitators of Christ, "the spiritual Rock that follows"[30] those who are being saved, in order that they may drink from it the "spiritual drink."[31] These bear the name rock, as does Christ. Being also "members of Christ,"[32] they bear the name "Christs" and as rocks "Peters." . . . [In the statement] "You are Peter" and the following up to "shall not prevail against it,"[33] what is the "it"? The rock upon which Christ builds the church or

27. Mark 3:17.
28. Matt 16:18.
29. Matt 16:19; cf. 18:18.
30. 1 Cor 10:4.
31. 1 Cor 10:4.
32. 1 Cor 6:15.
33. Matt 16:18.

the church (for the saying is ambiguous) or the rock and the church as one and the same? This I think is true. For the gates of Hades will prevail against neither the rock upon which Christ builds the church nor the church. . . . If the gates of Hades will prevail against anyone, that person would not be a rock upon which Christ builds the church nor the church built by Christ on the rock. . . . The church as the building of Christ who wisely built his own house upon the rock[34] is inaccessible to the gates of Hades, which prevail over every person who is outside the rock and the church but have no power against it.

34. Matt 7:24.

14

Cyprian

Cyprian came from an upper-class family in Carthage of the Roman province of (North) Africa. Converted to Christ as an adult in 245/246, his social standing and abilities led to his election as bishop of Carthage in 248. He went into exile during the Decian persecution, but then became a martyr under Valerian in 258. Cyprian's *Letters* and treatises are major sources for church history in the crucial time of the persecutions and controversies of the mid-third century. Cyprian was a key figure in controversies of his time that affected the churches: whether those who denied the faith in times of persecution could be readmitted to the fellowship of the church and if so on what terms, differences that created schisms in several churches; the schism in the church at Rome led by Novatian in opposition to the election of Cornelius as bishop; and the validity of baptisms and ordinations performed in schismatic and heretical bodies. The church at large supported Cyprian's policy of allowing apostates to be restored to communion on performing penance according to the gravity of the transgression and of recognizing Cornelius as bishop of Rome, but it did not follow him in requiring those baptized outside the catholic church to be rebaptized on seeking membership in it.

In the context of divisions prompted by these issues, Cyprian penned the first extant treatise on the nature of the church, *On the Unity of the Church*. He centered the unity of the church on the bishops. He viewed the episcopate as a corporate whole, with each local bishop sharing equally in the office that went back to Peter and the apostles. The text is preserved in two editions, both likely derived from Cyprian himself.

Cyprian presents the church as the pure bride of Christ. To forsake the church for a schismatic body is to become an adulteress. The promises of Christ are for the church; hence there are dire consequences for departing from the church. In this context, Cyprian makes his famous declaration that one cannot have God for Father who does not have the church for mother.[1] Cyprian draws on the common use of the ark of Noah as an image of the church to make the argument that outside the church there is no salvation.[2] He further saw the undivided robe of Jesus[3] as a symbol of the unity of the church that should not be torn asunder.

On the Unity of the Church 1–27[4]

1. Since the Lord warns and says, "you are the salt of the earth"[5] and since he orders us to be simple and innocent and

1. Cyprian, *On the Unity of the Church* 6; and *Letter* 74.7.
2. Cyprian, *Letter* 73.21.
3. John 19:23–24.
4. Adapted from Hinson, *Understandings of the Church*, 69–86.
5. Matt 5:13.

yet prudent in our simplicity, what is more fitting, dear friends, than to keep our eyes open and watching with anxious heart to understand the deceptions of the crafty enemy and beware lest we who have put on Christ, the Wisdom of God the Father, seem less than wise in guarding our salvation? For we must not fear only persecution and things that proceed by open assault to ruin and destroy the servants of God. Caution is easier where fear is evident, and the mind prepares itself for conflict when the adversary declares himself. An enemy must be feared and guarded against more when he creeps in secretly, when he crawls in by secret openings while deceiving one under the image of peace. From this he gets the name of serpent. That is always his cunning. That is the blind and secret deception for ensnaring a person. Thus from the beginning of the world on has he deceived. Flattering with lying words, he has deceived the uninstructed soul by careless credulity. Thus when he attempted to tempt the Lord himself, he came upon him secretly, as if he might creep up on him a second time and deceive him. Nevertheless, he was spotted and beaten back and indeed knocked down because he was recognized and unmasked.

2. From this we were given an example that we should flee the way of the old humanity and walk in the footsteps of the conquering Christ, lest carelessly we return again into the trap of death rather than attain to the immortality won for us by foreseeing the danger. Yet how can we attain immortality unless we keep the commandments of Christ by which death is fought and overcome? Christ himself warns and says, "If you want to enter into life, keep the commandments."[6] And again, "If you do what I command you, I no longer will call you servants but friends."[7] Indeed, he calls strong and firm those

6. Matt 19:17.

who are founded securely upon a rock, who stand fixed with immovable and unshaken firmness against all the tempests and winds of the age. "Who hears my words and does them," he says, "I will compare to a wise man who builds his house upon a rock. The rain fell, the floods came, the winds blew and beat against that house, and it did not fall. For it was founded upon a rock."[8]

We ought therefore to stand upon, learn, and do his words, whatever he both taught and did. How else can anyone say that she believes in Christ who does not do what Christ commanded us to do? Or how will she attain the reward of faith who does not want to keep faith with the commandments? Such a person must of necessity totter and go astray and, seized by the spirit of error, be whirled like dust that the wind blows up. One who does not hold the truth of the way of salvation will not advance in his walk to salvation.

3. We must beware, dear friends, not only of what is open and evident but also of cunning trickery and subtle deceit. What is more cunning or more subtle than that the enemy who was unmasked and knocked down at the advent of Christ—after light came to the gentiles and the sun poured out its light for the salvation of humankind, so that the deaf received news of the grace of the Spirit, the blind opened their eyes to God, the weak grew strong with eternal health, the lame ran to the church, the deaf prayed with clear voices and prayers—seeing idols abandoned and his seats and temples deserted by a wonderful number of believers, should think up a new deception that he might deceive the careless under the very title of the name "Christian"? He invented heresies and schisms by which he might subvert the faith, corrupt the truth,

7. John 15:14, 15.
8. Matt 7:24–25.

and rend the unity of the church. Those he cannot hold to the blindness of the old way he surrounds and deceives by leading them astray on a new road. He snatches people from the church itself and, just as they seem to have drawn near to the light and to have escaped the world's night, he pulls the shades down again. So those standing neither with the gospel of Christ nor its observance and law call themselves Christians. Walking in darkness, they think they have the light. The Adversary flatters and deceives. He is the one who, according to the word of the apostle, changes himself into an angel of light and adorns his servants like servants of righteousness. The latter declare that night is day, death salvation, despair a garb for hope, infidelity a pretext for faith, antichrist the same as Christ, so that they render truth useless by the subtle use of plausible lies. This is what happens, dear friends, when we do not return to the source of truth nor seek the head nor keep the teaching of the heavenly teacher.

4. If anyone ponders and weighs these things, there is no need for a long discussion and argument. It is easy to prove the faith by a summary of the truth. The Lord says to Peter: "I tell you that you are Peter, and upon this rock I will build my church, and the gates of hell will not overcome it. I will give you the keys of the kingdom of heaven, and whatever you bind on earth will be bound also in heaven, and whatever you loose on earth will be loosed also in heaven."[9] And again he says to him after the resurrection: "Feed my sheep."[10] Now he shares his power equally with all the apostles after his resurrection, saying: "Just as the Father has sent me, I also send you. Receive my Holy Spirit. If you forgive the sins of anyone, they will

9. Matt 16:18–19.

10. John 21:15. A later edition added: "He builds his church upon that one, and commands him to feed his sheep."

be forgiven; if you retain the sins of anyone, they will be retained."[11] Nevertheless, in order to make unity evident, by his own authority he arranged for the source of this same unity to begin with one person. The other apostles were without doubt what Peter was, endowed with an equal partnership of honor and power, but the beginning proceeds from unity [Peter] so that the church of Christ might be shown to be one.[12] In the Song of Songs also the Holy Spirit signifies that the church is one from the person of the Lord, saying: "One is my dove, my perfect one. She is her mother's only one, the choice one of the one who begot her."[13] Does a person who does not keep this unity of the church believe that he keeps the faith? Does a person who battles and resists the church [the later edition adds: "who deserts the chair of Peter upon which the church was founded"] have confidence that he is in the church when the blessed apostle Paul teaches the same thing and shows the mystery of the unity, saying: "There is one body and one spirit, one hope of your calling, one Lord, one faith, one baptism, one God"?[14]

5. This unity we must firmly maintain and affirm, especially we bishops who superintend the church, so that we may demonstrate that the episcopate is one and indivisible. Let no one deceive the brotherhood with a lie. Let no one corrupt the truth of faith with a faithless sham. The episcopate is one, a part of which is held in its entirety by an individual. One is the church, which is extended far and wide by the increase of her fruitfulness, in the same way as there are many rays of the sun but one light and many branches of a tree but one

11. John 20:20–23.
12. The later edition adds: "And primacy is given Peter, so that one church of Christ and one chair of the bishop may be shown. All are pastors, but one flock is shown which is fed by all the apostles with unanimous agreement."
13. Song 6:9.
14. Eph 4:4–6.

strength founded in a sturdy root. When many streams flow from one spring, although the number seems to be increased by the amount of water pouring out, still unity is preserved at the source. Pluck a ray of sun from the body; its unity allows no division of the light. Break a branch from a tree; broken, it will not be able to bud. Cut off a stream from the spring; cut off, it dries up. So too the church, glowing with the light of the Lord, extends her rays over the whole world; nevertheless it is one light that is diffused everywhere, nor is the unity of the body divided. With her rich supply, she extends her branches throughout the earth, wider and wider she expands her rippling streams. Yet there is one head and one source and one mother who is endlessly fertile. We are born from her womb, nourished by her milk, and animated by her spirit.

6. It is not possible for the spouse of Christ to be adulterous. She is uncorrupted and chaste. She knows one home; she guards the sanctity of one bedroom with pure chastity. She keeps us for God; she seals for the kingdom the sons whom she bore. Whoever separates from the church and is joined to an adulteress is separated from the promises of the church, nor does one who forsakes the church of Christ arrive at the rewards of Christ. That person is an alien, is profane, is an enemy. It is not possible for a person to have God any longer as Father who does not have the church as mother. If anyone who was outside the ark of Noah was able to escape, also the one who is outside the church may escape. The Lord warns and says, "Whoever is not with me is against me, and one who does not gather with me scatters."[15] One who breaks the peace and harmony of Christ acts against Christ. One who gathers elsewhere outside the church scatters. The Lord says, "I and the Father are one."[16] And again it is written concerning the

15. Matt 12:30.

Father and the Son and the Holy Spirit, "And these three are one."[17] Does anyone believe that this unity, which comes from divine strength and is united in celestial mysteries, can be split in the church and cut off by the divorce of clashing wills? One who does not keep this unity does not keep God's law, nor faith in the Father and Son, nor life and salvation.

7. This mystery[18] of unity, this bond of harmony held together inseparably, is shown when in the Gospel the coat of the Lord Jesus Christ was not divided in any way nor torn, but when they cast lots for the garment of Christ (as to who should put on Christ), the garment was received whole and undamaged and the coat was possessed undivided.[19] The divine Scripture says, "But because his robe was not sewn from above but was woven throughout, they said to one another: 'Let us not split it, but let us cast lots for it to determine who gets it.'"[20] It bore the unity that comes "from above," that is, which comes from heaven and from the Father, which could not be split at all by taking and possessing it but kept its complete and firm strength without division. It is not possible for the person who tears and divides the church of Christ to possess the garment of Christ. On the contrary, when, as Solomon was dying, his kingdom and people were split, Ahijah the prophet met King Jeroboam in the field and tore his clothing into twelve pieces, saying, "You take ten pieces because the Lord says: 'Behold, I am splitting the kingdom from the hand of Solomon and I will give you ten scepters. And he will have two scepters for the sake of my servant David and for the sake of the city of Jerusalem, which I have chosen to put my name there.'"[21]

16. John 10:30.
17. 1 John 5:7.
18. *Sacramentum.*
19. John 19:23–24.
20. John 19:23–24.
21. 1 Kgs 11:31–32.

When the twelve tribes of Israel were being split, the prophet Ahijah divided his clothing. Since the people of Christ cannot be torn into two, his coat, woven and held together as a whole, was not divided by those who possessed it. In one piece, closely connected, joined together—the coat showed our people, who have put on Christ, hold together in harmony. By the mystery[22] and sign of his garment he declared the unity of the church.

8. Who, then, is so wicked and treasonous, so crazy with the fury of discord, as either to believe the unity of the church, the garment of the Lord, the church of Christ, can be split or to dare to split it? Christ warns in his Gospel and teaches, saying, "And there will be one flock and one shepherd."[23] Does anyone think there can be in one place either many shepherds or many flocks? Likewise, the apostle Paul, urging this same unity upon us, begs and urges, saying, "I beg you, brothers and sisters, by the name of our Lord Jesus Christ, that all of you say the same thing and that there be no schisms among you, but that you may be joined together in the same mind and in the same thoughts."[24] And he says also, "Hold one another up in love, striving to keep the unity of the Spirit in the bond of peace."[25] Do you think one can stand and live when one withdraws from the church and establishes other chairs and different houses for himself, since it was said to Rahab, in whom the church was prefigured: "Gather your father and your mother and your brothers and the entire household of your father into your own home with yourself, and everyone who goes outside the door of your house will be liable for himself"?[26] Similarly, the sacrament of the Passover in the book of Exodus contains

22. *Sacramentum.*
23. John 10:16.
24. 1 Cor 1:10.
25. Eph 4:2–3.
26. Josh 2:18–19.

nothing else than that the lamb, which is killed as a type of Christ, be eaten in one house. God says, "It will be eaten in one house; you will not throw the flesh outside the house."[27] The flesh of Christ and the holy thing of the Lord cannot be thrown outside, and there is no home for believers except the one church. The Holy Spirit marks clearly this house, this inn of unanimity, in the Psalms, saying, "God, who makes us live together in unanimity in one house."[28] In the house of God, in the church of Christ they live in unanimity. They continue in harmony and simplicity.

9. This is also why the Holy Spirit comes in the dove. It is a simple and joyous creature, not bitter with gall, not fierce and apt to bite, not ready to rip one with violent claws. It loves human hospitality and knows the fellowship of one home. When they bear offspring, they bring them up together. When they fly about, they stay with one another in flight. They spend their lives in united behavior. They acknowledge the harmony of peace with a mutual kiss. They fulfill the law of unanimity in all things. This is the simplicity that must be known in the church, the love which must be practiced, so that the love of the brotherhood may imitate the doves and kindliness and gentleness be equal to those of lambs and sheep. What place has the ferocity of wolves and the madness of dogs and the deadly poison of snakes and the cruel fury of wild animals in the breast of Christians? We must rejoice when such persons are separated from the church lest they prey upon the doves or the sheep of Christ with their cruel and poisonous contact. Bitterness cannot be united and mixed with sweetness, darkness with light, storm with calm, war with peace, sterility with fertility, drought with springs of water, tempest with

27. Exod 12:46.
28. Ps 68:8.

tranquility. Let no one think that good persons can leave the church. Wind does not blow away the grain, nor does a hurricane overturn a deeply rooted tree. It is the empty husks that are blown away by the tempest, and feeble trees that are overturned by the twisting of the whirlwind. John the apostle curses and strikes these, saying, "They went out from us, but they were not of us. If they had been of us, they would certainly have remained with us."[29]

10. Hence heresies have frequently occurred and still occur, since a perverted mind has no peace and discordant perfidy does not keep unity. But the Lord permits and allows this to happen, inasmuch as each person's will remains free, so that while the test of truth searches our hearts and our minds, the sound faith of those who are proven may shine with a clear light. Through the apostle the Holy Spirit warns us, saying, "There must be heresies so that those who are proven may be evident among you."[30] In this manner the faithful are proven, the faithless are unmasked, and the souls of the just and the unjust are distinguished already before the judgment day and the husks are separated from the wheat. The latter are the ones who install themselves over their rash associates without divine appointment, who appoint themselves as bishops without any law of ordination, who take the name of the bishops without anyone giving them the episcopate. In the Psalms, the Holy Spirit describes them as "sitting in the chair of pestilence."[31] They are plagues and blights on the faith, deceiving with the mouth of the serpent and vomiting out deadly poisons with plague-bearing tongues as devices for corrupting the truth, whose word "crawls like a cancer"[32] and

29. 1 John 2:19.
30. 1 Cor 11:19.
31. Ps 1:1.
32. 2 Tim 2:17.

whose writing pours a deadly virus into the breasts and hearts of individuals.

11. Against people of this type the Lord cries out. He holds his erring people back from them and recalls them, saying, "Don't listen to the words of the false prophets since the visions of their heart invalidate them. They speak, but not from the mouth of the Lord. They say to those who throw away the word of God: 'You and all those who proceed according to their own wills will have peace. No evil will happen to anyone who proceeds in the error of his heart.' I have not spoken to them; yet they themselves have prophesied. If they had stood in my council [substantia] and listened to my words and taught my people, I would have turned them from their evil thoughts."[33] The Lord again calls attention to these same persons, saying, "They have forsaken me, the fountain of living water, and dug out for themselves cracked cisterns that cannot hold water."[34] When there cannot be more than one baptism, they think they can baptize. Having deserted the fountain of life, they promise the gift of living and saving water. People are not cleansed there; rather, they are defiled. Sins are not purged there; rather, they are piled higher. That "birth" bears children not for God but for the devil. Born through a lie, they do not lay hold on the promises of the truth. Procreated from faithlessness, they lose the gift of faith. They who have shattered the peace of the Lord with the fury of discord cannot come to the reward of peace.

12. Let certain persons not deceive themselves with empty interpretation of the Lord's statement that "wherever two or three are gathered in my name, I am with them."[35] Corrupters

33. Jer 23:16–21.
34. Jer 2:13.
35. Matt 18:20.

and false interpreters of the gospel put down the last part and glide over the first, mindful of one part but deceitfully suppressing the other. Just as they have themselves split the church, so they split the meaning of one passage. For the Lord was urging agreement and peace among his disciples. "I tell you," he says, "that if two of you agree about anything on earth, whatever you ask will be granted you by my Father, who is in heaven. For wherever two or three are gathered in my name, I am with them."[36] This shows that most is given not for the great number but for the agreement of those who pray. "If two of you will agree on earth," he says. He put agreement first. He put peaceful harmony first. He taught us to agree faithfully and firmly. But how can one agree with someone who does not agree with Christ's body, the church, and with the whole brotherhood? How can two or three gather in the name of Christ when they are separated from Christ and from his gospel? For we have not withdrawn from them; rather, they have withdrawn from us, since heresies and schisms have been born later when they established separate meetings for themselves and abandoned the head and source of truth. However, the Lord tells his church and those who are in the church that they can obtain what they ask from the divine majesty if they agree, if they pray with one mind when two or three gather as he commanded and advised. "Wherever two or three are gathered in my name," he says, "I am with them," that is, with the simple and peaceful, with those who fear God and keep God's commandments. He said he is with those "two or three" especially when he was with the three children in the fiery furnace. Because they remained simple toward God and of one mind among themselves, he refreshed their spirits in the midst of the flames that encircled them "with the spirit

36. Matt 18:20.

of dew." In like manner, he was present with the two apostles when they were shut up in prison because they were simple and of one mind. When the prison doors were opened, he placed them again in the marketplace that they might deliver the Word, which they preached faithfully to the crowd. When he places among his precepts the statement, "where two or three are gathered in my name, I am with them," therefore, he does not divide people from the church, he who established and created the church. Rather, reproving the faithless for discord and commending the faithful for peace with his own voice, he shows that he is more fully present with two or three praying with one mind than with many schismatics and that more can be obtained by the harmonious petition of a few than by the unharmonious prayer of many.

13. When he gave the rule of prayer, moreover, he added: "And when you stand and pray, forgive whatever you hold against someone so that your Father who is in heaven may forgive you your sins."[37] And he recalls a person going to the altar to offer a sacrifice with discord in his heart and orders him first to be reconciled with his brother and then to return with peace to make an offering to God. For God did not look with favor on Cain's offering, for one who did not have peace with his brother on account of the divisiveness of jealousy could not have God at peace with him. What son of peace, then, do those who hate brothers and sisters promise themselves? What kind of sacrifices do those who envy the priests think they celebrate? Or do those who gather outside the church of Christ think that Christ is with them when they gather?

14. Though such persons should be slain confessing the name, this stain is not washed away even by blood. Responsibility for discord is so grave and inexpiable it cannot

37. Mark 11:25.

be washed away even by suffering. A person who is not in the church cannot be a martyr. One who forsakes her who is about to reign could never attain to the kingdom. Christ gave us peace. He taught us to be agreeable and of one mind. He commanded that the bonds of love and charity be kept uncorrupted and undefiled. One who has not kept fraternal love, therefore, cannot claim martyrdom. The apostle Paul teaches and attests this when he says, "And if I have such faith as to move mountains but do not have love, I am nothing. And if I give all my possessions to feed the poor and surrender my body to be burned, but do not have love, I am not benefited. Love is patient. Love is kind. Love does not envy. It does not behave improperly. It is not puffed up. It is not irritable. It does not think evil. It loves everything, believes everything, hopes everything, endures everything. Love never fails."[38] "Love," he says, "never fails." For it will always be in the kingdom. It will last forever in the unity of a brotherhood that holds together in itself. Discord can never attain to the kingdom of heaven, to the rewards of Christ, who said, "This is my commandment, that you love one another just as I have loved you."[39] One who has defiled the love of Christ with faithless schism could not fulfill this. A person who does not have love does not have God. Listen to the blessed apostle John. "God is love," he says. "Who abides in love abides in God, and God abides in that person."[40] They cannot abide with God who are not of one mind in the church of God. Though they give themselves up to burn in flames of fire or lay down their lives as prey for wild animals, they will not have the crown of faith but the penalty of faithlessness, nor the glorious end of religious virtue

38. 1 Cor 13:2–5, 7–8.
39. John 15:12.
40. 1 John 4:16.

but a death of despair. Such a person can be killed but not crowned. She may profess that she is a Christian as the devil often pretends to be Christ. As the Lord himself forewarns, "Many will come in my name, saying, 'I am the Christ,' and they will deceive many."[41] Just as that person is not Christ, even though she deceives in the name, so also one who does not persist in the truth of his gospel and of faith cannot be regarded as a Christian.

15. Although it is a high and wonderful thing certainly to prophesy and to cast out demons and to perform great miracles on earth, one who possesses all these gifts does not attain the heavenly kingdom unless that person walks on the straight and just road. The Lord declares that when he says, "For many will say to me on that day, 'Lord, Lord, have we not prophesied in your name and cast out demons in your name and performed great miracles in your name?' And then I will say to them, 'I do not know you. Depart from me, you who do evil.'"[42] Justice is needed if one is to find mercy before God as judge. His precepts and warnings must be obeyed if we are to receive mercy for our merits. When the Lord was pointing out in his gospel the way of our hope and faith with a brief summary, he says, "The Lord, your God, is one God," and "Love the Lord, your God, with all your heart and all your soul and all your strength." This is the first commandment. And the second is like it: "Love your neighbor as yourself. On these two commandments hang the law and the prophets."[43] In his teaching he taught both unity and love. He summarized all the Prophets and the Law in two commandments. But how does one preserve unity, how does one guard or think about

41. Mark 13:6.
42. Matt 7:22–23.
43. Mark 12:29–31.

love, who, crazy with the rage of discord, splits the church, destroys the faith, disturbs the peace, weakens love, profanes the sacrament?

16. The evil, faithful friends, began long ago. But now its cruel havoc has increased and the poisonous plague of heretical perversity and schisms have begun to arise and gain vigor. For that is what has to happen at the end of the world, as the Holy Spirit prophesies and forewarns us through the apostle. "In the last days," he says, "grievous times will come. People will be self-serving, proud, puffed up, covetous, blasphemers, disobedient to parents, ungrateful, impious, without natural affection, implacable, informers, unchaste, harsh, not loving good, traitors, wanton, inflated with folly, lovers of pleasure rather than God, holding the form of religion but denying its power. Some of them are the ones who sneak into homes and prey on foolish women burdened by sins who are led by various desires, always burning and yet never able to arrive at a knowledge of the truth. Just as Jannes and Jambres opposed Moses, so also these oppose the truth. But they will not go much farther, for their foolishness will be evident to all, just as theirs was."[44] Whatever was foretold is now fulfilled. As the end of the world approaches, it will come about equally for a testing of both human beings and times. As the adversary rages more and more, error deceives, folly extols, envy kindles, greed blinds, wickedness corrupts, pride puffs us, discord causes bitterness, anger plunges recklessly on.

17. Yet the excessive and sudden unfaithfulness of many should not move or disturb us, but rather it should confirm our faith in the truth of the matter which has been declared ahead of time. When some begin to be such because it was predicted, let other brothers and sisters beware of persons

44. 2 Tim 3:1–9.

of that type because it has also been predicted beforehand, as the Lord instructs, "But you beware. Lo, I have told you everything beforehand."[45] I beg you, brothers and sisters, avoid such persons, and remove your heart and ears as far as you can from such dangerous discussion, like contact with death, as it is written: "Hedge your ears with thorns, and don't listen to an evil tongue."[46] And again: "Evil conversation corrupts good manners."[47] The Lord teaches and admonishes us to withdraw from such. "The blind," he says, "are leaders of the blind. But if a blind person leads a blind person, both fall into a ditch."[48] Whoever has become separated from the church must be shunned and fled from. This type of person is perverted, sins, and is self-condemned. Or does a person who acts against Christ's priests and withdraws himself from the company of his clergy and people seem to be with Christ himself? That person bears arms against the church and fights against the ordinance of God. An enemy of the altar, a rebel against Christ's sacrifice, a traitor to the faith, a blasphemer of religion, a disobedient servant, a wicked son, a hostile brother—this person dares to despise the bishops and forsake God's priests and set up another altar, to profane the truth of the Lord's offering by false sacrifices. He does not know that anyone who struggles against the ordinance of God is punished by divine chastisement on account of his reckless audacity.

18. Thus Korah, Dathan, and Abiram paid penalties immediately for their efforts to claim for themselves the right to sacrifice as priests in opposition to Moses and Aaron. Its bonds broken, the earth opened up into a deep cave, and the hole in the gaping soil swallowed them alive where they stood.

45. Mark 13:23.
46. Cf. Sir 28:24–26.
47. 1 Cor 15:33.
48. Matt 15:14.

The wrath of an angry God struck not only those who were responsible for this, but the strange fire streaming from the Lord also consumed with quick vengeance the two hundred and fifty other participants and allies in this same uprising who were cohorts with them in this audacity. This warns and shows, of course, that whatever wicked deeds were attempted by human will in order to destroy the ordinance of God are done in opposition to God. So, too, King Uzziah was confounded by the divine wrath and defiled by a kind of leprosy on his forehead when he carried the censer and violently took upon himself the offering of a sacrifice contrary to the law of God, despite the opposition of Azariah the priest, and would not yield and withdraw. He was branded by the offended Lord on the part of the body where those who obtain the favor of the Lord are sealed. The sons of Aaron, who placed strong fire on the altar, which the Lord did not command, were immediately blotted out in the sight of the avenging Lord.

19. Those who seek strange doctrines and introduce teachings devised by human beings, despising what God has handed down, are the ones whom they naturally imitate and follow. The Lord rebukes and castigates them in his Gospel, saying, "You reject the commandment of God so that you may establish your own tradition."[49] This is a worse offense than those who fell in persecution seem to have committed, yet who do penance for that offense and entreat God, making full satisfaction. In the latter the church is sought and asked for; in the former it is combatted. In one case there may have been the use of force; in the other the will is gripped by wickedness. In one case the one who has fallen has harmed only himself; in the other one who has tried to make a heresy or schism deceives many and drags them down with himself. In one case

49. Mark 7:9.

there is loss of one soul, in the other danger for many. Certainly the lapsed person understands that he has sinned and laments and weeps about it. The other person, puffed up in his breast and pleased with his own sins, separates children from their mother, solicits sheep from their shepherd, and upsets the mysteries of God. Although the lapsed sinned once, this person sins daily. Finally, the lapsed person who has obtained martyrdom later can receive the promises of the kingdom, but this person, should he be killed outside the church, cannot attain to the rewards that belong to the church.

20. No one should be amazed, dear brothers and sisters, that some of the confessors have reached the point that some of them also sin so wickedly and grievously. Not even confession makes one immune to the devil's tricks or safeguards one living in the world with perpetual security against worldly temptations, dangers, attacks, and assaults. Otherwise we would never again see among confessors deceptions, fornication, and adultery such as we now are grieving about among some. Whoever the confessor, that person is not greater or better or dearer to God than Solomon. As long as he walked in the paths of the Lord, he was endowed with grace he had received from the Lord. Yet after he abandoned the way of the Lord, he also lost the grace of the Lord. Moreover, it is written: "Hold on to what you have lest another take your crown."[50] Certainly the Lord would not threaten that he might take away the crown of righteousness unless when justice goes, the crown must go too.

21. Confession is the beginning of glory; it does not deserve a crown at once. It does not perfect praise, but it imitates honor, for it is written: "Whoever perseveres to the end will be saved."[51] Whatever has preceded the end is a step by which one

50. Rev 3:11.

climbs to the summit of salvation. It is not the end where the highest peak is reached. One is a confessor, but after confession the danger is greater, for the adversary has been provoked more. If one is a confessor, that person ought to stand still more firmly with the gospel of the Lord, inasmuch as she has obtained glory from the Lord through the gospel. For the Lord says, "Much is required of one who is given much, and more service is demanded of one to whom greater honor is ascribed."[52] Let no one perish because of the example of a confessor. Let no one learn injustice, insolence, or unfaithfulness from a confessor's behavior. If one is a confessor, that person should be humble, peaceable, modest, and disciplined in conduct, so that whoever is called a confessor of Christ may imitate the Christ she confesses. For Christ says, "Whoever exalts himself will be humbled and whoever humbles himself will be exalted."[53] Because the Word and Power and Wisdom of God, the Father, humbled himself on earth, he has himself been exalted. How, then, can he love exaltation, who commanded us in his law to be humble and himself received from the Father a most excellent name as a prize for humility? One is a confessor of Christ only if the majesty and dignity of Christ are not blasphemed later by him. Let not the tongue that has confessed Christ speak evil or be disruptive. Let it not be heard to rumble with abuses and quarrels. Let it not spew out the poison of a serpent against brothers and priests of God after words of praise. If one should afterward become culpable and hateful, waste his confession by evil behavior, defile his life by base filthiness, and finally, exchange his original faith for later faithlessness, forsaking

51. Matt 10:22.
52. Luke 12:48.
53. Luke 18:14.

the church in which he became a confessor and splitting the harmony of unity, that person cannot flatter himself on the basis of his confession by thinking he has been chosen for the prize of glory when, for this very reason, he deserves punishments all the more.

22. The Lord chose Judas to be one of the apostles, yet Judas later betrayed the Lord. Even so, the firm faith of the apostle did not fail because the traitor Judas defected from this company. Similarly, in this case also, the holiness and dignity of the confessors have not been immediately diminished because the faith of some of them has been shattered. The blessed apostle Paul says in his letter, "What if some of them fell from the faith? Has their unfaithfulness destroyed the effectiveness of God's faithfulness? Never! For God is true, even if every human being is a liar."[54] The larger and better part of the confessors stands fast in the strength of their faith and in the truth of the Lord's law and teaching. They do not depart from the peace of the church who are mindful that they have obtained grace in the church by virtue of God's favor. For this reason they obtain fuller praise for their faith because, separated from the faithlessness of those who were fellow confessors, they have drawn back from contact with the offense. But illuminated by the light of the gospel and suffused with the pure and white light of the Lord, they are as worthy of praise for preserving the peace of Christ as they have been victorious in their encounter with the devil.

23. Dear brothers and sisters, my desire, my counsel, and my plea is that, if possible, not one of the brothers and sisters be lost and that the rejoicing mother may draw to her bosom one body of people who agree with one another. Yet if this saving counsel could not recall to the way of salvation some leaders of

54. Rom 3:3–4.

the schisms and creators of factions who persist in their blind and obstinate madness, at least you others, who have either been caught through naïveté or led into error or deceived by some very clever trick, should free yourselves from the snares of deceit, liberate your wandering steps from errors, and recognize the right way to heaven. The voice of the apostle bears witness. "We command you in the name of our Lord Jesus Christ," he says, "to withdraw from all brothers and sisters who proceed in a disorderly way and not according to the tradition that they received from us."[55] And again he says, "Let no one deceive you by empty words, for the wrath of God is coming upon the children of disobedience for this reason. Don't get involved with them, therefore."[56] We must withdraw or rather flee from those who stray lest, if anyone joins those who behave badly and walks down the path of error and crime, that person wander from the true path and also become liable for the same crime. There is one God, one Christ, one church of Christ, one faith, and a people fastened together in solid corporate unity by the glue of concord. This unity cannot be split nor the one body divided by tearing up the structure. It cannot be broken into fragments by tearing and mangling its viscera. Whatever has been separated from the womb cannot live and breathe outside it; it loses the essence of health.

24. The Holy Spirit warns us, saying, "Who is it who wants life and loves to see the best days? Restrain your tongue from evil, and let not your lips speak deceptively. Avoid evil and do good. Seek peace and pursue it."[57] A child of peace ought to seek peace and pursue it. Whoever knows and loves the bond of love ought to restrain her tongue from the evil of faction.

55. 2 Thess 3:6.
56. Eph 5:6–7.
57. Ps 34:13–15; 1 Pet 3:10–11.

Among his divine commandments and salutary teaching, as he approached his death, the Lord added this: "Peace I leave with you. My peace I give you."[58] He gave us this inheritance. He promised all his pledged gifts and rewards for the keeping of peace. If we are heirs of Christ, let us remain in the peace of Christ. If we are children of God, we ought to be peacemakers. "Blessed are the peacemakers," he says, "for they will be called children of God."[59] Children of God ought to be peacemakers, gentle in heart, simple in speech, agreeable in affection, faithfully binding themselves together with the words of unanimity.

25. Such unanimity once existed under the apostles. In this manner the new company of believers, keeping the Lord's commandments, preserved its love. This is proven by the divine Scripture, which says: "And the multitude of those who believed were acting with one soul and mind."[60] And again: "And they were all persisting with one mind in prayer with the women and Mary, the mother of Jesus, and his brothers."[61] For that reason they were praying effective prayers and could obtain with confidence whatever they asked of the Lord's mercy.

26. But among us unanimity has diminished just as liberality in good deeds has been broken. In those days they were selling their houses and farms, and laying up treasures for themselves in heaven; they were offering the proceeds to the apostles to be distributed for the use of the needy. But now we do not even give a tithe from our patrimony, and we buy and increase our possessions rather than selling them as the Lord ordered. As a result, the vigor of faith has dried up among us

58. John 14:27.
59. Matt 5:9.
60. Acts 4:32.
61. Acts 1:14.

and the strength of believers has grown faint. Therefore the Lord, looking at our times, says in his Gospel: "Do you think the Son of man will find faith on earth when he comes?"[62] We see that what he predicted has happened. There is no faith in the fear of the Lord, in the law of righteousness, in love, in work. No one thinks about fear of things to come. No one meditates on the Day of the Lord, the wrath of God, the punishment about to befall the unbeliever, and the eternal torments established for unbelief. Our conscience does not fear what it would fear if it believed because it doesn't believe at all. If it believed, it would also fear. If it feared, it would escape.

27. Let us arouse ourselves as much as we can, dear brothers and sisters, break off the slumber of our old sloth, and keep our eyes open to observe and carry out the Lord's commands. Let us be the kind of persons he commanded us to be when he says: "Let your loins be girded and your lights burning, and you be like people waiting for their Lord when he returns from the wedding so that they may open to him when he comes and knocks. Blessed are those servants whom the Lord will find awake when he comes."[63] We ought to be girded up lest, when the day of the campaign comes, he find us hindered and unready. Let our light shine and gleam with good works that it may guide us out of this world's night to the light of eternal glory. Always careful and cautious, let us await the Lord's sudden advent so that, when he knocks, our faith may receive the prize of watchfulness from the Lord. If these commandments are kept and these warnings and precepts observed, we cannot be caught sleeping by the deceitful devil; we will reign with Christ as watchful servants.

62. Luke 18:8.
63. Luke 12:35–37.

15

Firmilian

Firmilian was bishop of Caesarea in Cappadocia from the early 230s to 268 and was prominent in church affairs during this period. He supported Cyprian of Carthage against Stephen of Rome on the nonacceptance of baptisms administered by those outside the communion of the catholic/orthodox church. His only surviving writing is a letter to Cyprian on this subject. It was preserved in Latin translation among the collection of Cyprian's correspondence. He likens the church, as others did, to the ark of Noah and to the enclosed garden of the Song of Songs.[1] He thus makes the same argument as Cyprian for the necessity of being in the unity of the church in order to be saved and that those baptized in a heretical body must receive baptism in the true church.

1. Song 4:12–15.

Firmilian in Cyprian, *Letters* 75.15

15.1. The church, according to the Song of Songs, is an enclosed garden, a sealed fountain, a paradise of fruit-bearing trees.[2] How shall they who have never entered into this garden nor seen the paradise planted by God the Creator be able to offer to another the living water of the saving bath[3] from the fountain enclosed within the garden and sealed with a divine seal?

15.2. The ark of Noah too was nothing else than the mystery[4] of the church of Christ. At that time when all on the outside were perishing, the ark kept safe only those who were within it. By this we are manifestly instructed to look to the unity of the church. Even so the apostle Peter said, "Thus also shall baptism in like manner make you safe,"[5] showing that as they who were not in the ark with Noah not only were not cleansed and saved by water but also perished in that deluge. So, now also, whoever are not in the church with Christ will perish outside, unless they turn by repentance to the one and only saving bath of the church.[6]

2. Song 4:12–15.
3. The original Greek would have been *loutron*, in Titus 3:5.
4. *Sacramentum* for the likely Greek *mysterion*.
5. 1 Pet 3:21.
6. Adapted from the translation by Ernest Wallis in *Fathers of the Third Century: Hippolytus, Cyprian, Caius, Novatian, Appendix*, ed. Alexander Roberts and James Donaldson, The Ante-Nicene Fathers (Buffalo, NY: Christian Literature, 1885–1896), 5:394.

16

Methodius

Methodius was bishop of Olympus in Lycia and died about 311. Most of his literary works are lost or survive only in a late translation into Old Church Slavonic. One extensive work to survive in Greek is the *Symposium*. In it ten virgins discuss in dialogue form ascetic spirituality. Methodius was a critic of Origen's theology, notably on the nature of the resurrection. He shared with Origen, however, an allegorical interpretation of Scripture and the images of the church as bride and mother.

Symposium 3.8.70–74

3.8.70. [Developing the theme of Adam as a type of Christ:] The apostle accurately referred to Christ the things said to Adam. For it is most certainly agreed that the church came into being out of his bones and his flesh. For this cause the Word left the Father in heaven and came down to be joined to his wife, slept in the ecstasy of his passion, and died willingly for her "in order that he might present to himself the church glorious and blameless, having purified her by the bath."[1] He did this so that she might receive the blessed spiritual seed that he sows by prompting and planting it in the depth of the mind. The church in the manner of a woman receives and gives form to the seed in order to give birth and nourishment to virtue.

3.8.71. The church could not otherwise conceive and give new birth to believers through the bath[2] unless Christ had emptied himself for their sake. . . . 3.8.72. This was in order that all those who have been built up in him might grow, namely, those who have been born through the bath from his bones and flesh, that is, receiving his holiness and his glory. . . .

3.8.74. For those who are the better and have indeed grasped the truth more clearly, these who on account of a perfect purification and faith have been withdrawn from the offenses of the flesh, become a church and "helper" of Christ, purified and given in marriage to him, a "virgin" according to the apostle,[3] in order that by receiving the pure and productive seed of his teaching they may become fellow workers and helpers in the preaching for the salvation of others.

Symposium 8.8.190–91

8.8.190. The enlightened[4] receive without modification the characteristics, the image, the manliness of Jesus. The form of the Word according to his likeness is stamped in them and is [191] generated in them according to an accurate knowledge and faith so that in each Christ is spiritually begotten.

On account of this, the church swells and is in birth pangs

1. Eph 5:26–27.
2. See Titus 3:5.
3. 2 Cor 11:2.
4. I.e., the baptized.

until Christ has been born and "is formed" in us[5] so that each of the saints may be born a christ by participating in Christ. This is borne out by the word in a certain Scripture, "Do not touch my anointed ones, and do no harm to my prophets,"[6] as if to say that those who have been baptized into Christ by participation in the Spirit have become christs. The church herein conceives by the Word their illumination and transformation.

5. Gal 4:19.
6. Ps 105:15 (104:15 Greek).

17

Eusebius

Eusebius was bishop of Caesarea in Palestine from about 313 to about 339. He is remembered especially as a historian for his ten-book *Church History* and as a supporter of the emperor Constantine for his *Life of Constantine*, but he was also a commentator on biblical books and a participant in theological discussions. He was also a notable apologist for Christianity, writing the *Preparation for the Gospel* and the *Proof of the Gospel*. Our quotation from early in the former apologetic work asserts the invincibility of the church, reflecting the triumph of Christianity under Constantine. Although Eusebius and others connected the Christian religion with the true worship of God from primordial times (for example, extensively in *Preparation for the Gospel* 7.1–11), in this passage he correctly notes that the church was not established during the lifetime of Jesus.

Preparation for the Gospel 1.3 (7d)

1.3 (7d). Therefore, he [our Savior] prophesied that his teaching would be preached throughout the whole world of human beings as a testimony to all nations, and by divine foreknowledge that the church later composed out of all nations by his own power, although not yet seen or established in the times he was in human form, would be unconquerable and undaunted and would be never conquered by death.[1] It stands and remains unshaken, as upon an unshaken and unbroken rock, established and rooted by his own power.

1. See Matt 16:18.

18

Athanasius

Athanasius was bishop of Alexandria from 328 to 373. He is remembered as the doughty champion of the creed adopted at the first ecumenical council at Nicaea in 325, which affirmed the full deity of Jesus Christ as "of the same substance" with God the Father and anathematized the teachings attributed to Arius that the Son of God was not coeternal with the Father and was a creature. Most of Athanasius's writings deal with the controversies surrounding the theological debates of his time.

Our first selection is from his *History of the Arians* and is not Athanasius's own words but a quotation from a letter of Hosius (or Ossius), bishop of Cordoba, to the emperor Constantius. Athanasius quotes the letter in his defense of Hosius, and the statements may be taken as representing Athanasius's own views on the respective spheres of the church and civil government. Such an affirmation of the separation of church and state was more often invoked by the party out of favor with the government at the given time, but the principle has been a standard in Christian thought.

Athanasius annually wrote a "festal letter" to the churches of Egypt announcing the date of the Pasch and giving instruction on whatever he thought needful at the time. Our second selection is from a later Latin quotation thought to be a fragment of his *Festal Letter* 29, for the year 357. The letter reflects the circumstance when the government took over church buildings from the supporters of Athanasius and delivered them to his doctrinal opponents. Hence, Athanasius affirms that the church is the people holding the true faith, not the place where they meet.

History of the Arians 6.44

6.44. [Hosius to Constantius:] Intrude not yourself into ecclesiastical matters, nor give commands to us concerning them, but learn them from us. God has put into your hands the kingdom; to us [clergy] he has entrusted the affairs of his church. As he who would steal the empire from you would resist the ordinance of God, so likewise fear on your part that by taking upon yourself the government of the church, you become guilty of a great offense. It is written, "Render to Caesar the things that are Caesar's and to God the things that are God's."[1] It is not permitted to us to exercise an earthly rule, nor have you, Sir, any authority to burn incense [that is, to exercise priestly functions].[2]

1. Matt 22:21.
2. Adapted from Archibald Robertson, trans., *Select Writings and Letters of Athanasius, Bishop of Alexandria*, Nicene and Post-Nicene Fathers (Buffalo, NY: Christian Literature, 1887–1894), second series, 4:286.

Festal Letter 29

29 (fragment). May God comfort you. I know moreover that not only this thing saddens you, but also the fact that while others have obtained the churches by violence, you are meanwhile cast out from your places. For they hold the places, but you the apostolic faith. They are, it is true, in the places, but outside the true faith; while you are outside the places indeed, but the faith is within you. Let us consider which is the greater, the place or the faith. Clearly, the true faith. Who then has lost more, or who possesses more? The one who holds the place, or the one who holds the faith? Good indeed is the place, when the apostolic faith is preached there; holy is it if the Holy One dwells there.[3]

3. Adapted from ibid., 4:550–51.

19

Cyril of Jerusalem

Cyril was appointed bishop of Jerusalem in 348. About that time, possibly while he was still a presbyter, he delivered a series of catechetical lectures to candidates preparing for baptism. These lectures were an exposition of the creed of the Jerusalem church. Several years later, he gave five mystagogical lectures on baptism, Eucharist, and chrism to the newly baptized, which have sometimes been attributed to his successor John of Jerusalem.

My selections are from the lecture on the article of the creed on "one holy catholic church, the resurrection of the flesh, and the life everlasting." Cyril was acutely aware of the presence of Jews and, like others, spoke negatively of them, now according to him displaced by Christians. He celebrated the triumph and spread of the church.

Cyril correctly defined the *ekklēsia* (church) as assembly, or gathering, and further identified it as a mother and a figure of the heavenly church. He advanced five reasons why the church is properly called the *katholikē* (catholic) church: it is spread throughout the world; it teaches completely all doctrines necessary for human knowledge; it submits the whole human race to godliness; it heals all classes of sins; and it possesses in itself every form of virtue.

Catechetical Lectures 18.24–25

18.24. It is well named "church" [*ekklēsia*], because all are called [*ekkaleisthai*] and gathered together. [There follow quotations of the word in Old Testament passages.] 25. . . . On account of the plots made against the Savior, the Jews were cast out from his grace. The Savior built out of the nations a second holy church composed of us Christians, concerning which he said to Peter, "And upon this rock I will build my church, and the gates of Hades shall not prevail against it."[1] . . . For now since the one church in Judea has been cast out, the churches of Christ are multiplied now in all the inhabited world.

Catechetical Lectures 18.26

Since the name of "church" [*ekklēsia*] is spoken concerning many different things, for instance as written concerning the crowd in the theater of the Ephesians [Acts 19:41] . . . , the faith delivered the article "one, holy, catholic church," in order that you may flee the foul gatherings [of heretics] and abide always in the holy catholic church in which you were regenerated. And if you sojourn in cities, do not inquire simply where the Lord's house is, for other impious heresies undertake to call their dens a house of the Lord. Nor inquire simply where is the church. Rather, ask, Where is the catholic church? For this is

1. Matt 16:18.

the proper name of this holy church and mother of us all. It is the bride of our Lord Jesus Christ, the one and only Son of God, . . . [Eph 5:25 quoted]. It is a type and copy of the Jerusalem above, which is free and mother of us all.[2] Formerly she was barren but now has many children.

Catechetical Lectures 18.23

[The church] is called "catholic,"[3] therefore, because it is in all the inhabited world, from one end of the earth to the other. Also, because it teaches universally and without omission all the doctrines that ought to come for human knowledge, concerning both things visible and invisible and things heavenly and earthly. Also, because it submits the whole human race to godliness, both rulers and those ruled, learned and unlearned. Also, because it heals and cures universally every kind of sins committed by soul and body. It possesses in itself every form of virtue that is named, in words and deeds and in every kind of spiritual gifts.

2. Gal 4:26.
3. *Katholikē*—universal, general.

20

Basil the Great

Basil came from a prominent Christian family, was well educated, and was a natural leader. He became bishop of Caesarea in Cappadocia 370–379. He resisted imperial efforts to impose a non-Nicene creed on the churches and worked for the unity of Greek and Latin churches.

Basil's voluminous correspondence provides rich information on society and church life in the fourth century. The first selection expresses Basil's earnest desire in a time of strife and trouble for peace and unity between the churches. The second selection reflects Basil's estimate of the deplorable condition of the churches as comparable to battles in war. He makes the battle a naval combat so he can add the aspect of a tempest on the sea to the conflict. Basil makes the observation that foes can be united because of a common enemy, but this union is shortlived. His *Letter* 92 similarly likens the controversies in the churches to warfare.

Authors and speakers often contrast present circumstances with a nostalgic remembrance of a good past. The third selection is likely Basil's exaggerated estimate of the way things once were, but it is a good statement of what was considered the ideal for the church.

The selection from Basil's homilies on the six days of creation moves in a somewhat different direction. After extolling the beauty of the sea and the usefulness of water, Basil praises the beauty of the assembly of the church, yet even here it is the harmony of persons of all ages and the calm that comes from faithfulness to the Lord.

Letter 156, to the Presbyter Evagrius

156.1. Is there anything more pleasing than the idea of peace? Is anything more fitting to the sacred office or more acceptable to the Lord than to endeavor to accomplish it? May you have the reward of the peacemaker. . . . My earnest desire and prayer is to see the day when those who are one in sentiment shall all fill the same assembly. Truly we would be the most outrageous of all persons if we rejoiced in schisms and divisions of the churches and did not consider the joining together of the members of the body of Christ to be the greatest of blessings. Know that our desire is as great as our power [to accomplish this] is deficient.

On the Holy Spirit 30.76–77

30.76. To what then shall I liken our present condition? It may be compared, I think, to a naval battle that has arisen out of longtime quarrels and is fought by men who cherish a deadly hate against one another, of long experience in naval warfare, and eager for the fight. . . . Consider, if you like, the ships driven back and forth by a raging storm, while thick darkness falls from the clouds and blackens all the scene, so that watchwords are indistinguishable in the confusion and all distinction between friend and foe is lost. . . . Jealousy of authority and the desire for individual mastery splits the sailors into parties that deal mutual death to one another. . . .

30.77. Turn now, I ask you, from this figurative description to the unhappy reality. . . . What storm at sea was ever so fierce and wild as this tempest of the churches? In it every landmark of the Fathers has been moved; every foundation, every bulwark of opinion has been shaken; everything buoyed up on the unsound is dashed about and shaken down. We attack one another. If our enemy is not the first to strike us, we are wounded by the comrade at our side. If a foe is stricken and falls, his fellow soldier tramples him down. There is at least this bond of union between us that we hate our common foes, but no sooner has the enemy gone than we find enemies in one another. . . . Already all the church is almost full of the inarticulate screams, the unintelligible noises, rising from the ceaseless agitations that divert the right rule of the doctrine of true religion, now in the direction of excess, now in that of defect.[1]

Letter 164 to Ascholius

164.1. [When we read your letter,] we thought we were back in olden times, when the churches of God flourished, rooted in the faith, united in love, when there existed a single agreement of the various members as in one body. Then the persecutors

1. Translation lightly adapted from Blomfield Jackson, trans., *The Treatise* De Spiritu Sancto, *the Nine Homilies of the Hexaemeron, and the Letters of Saint Basil the Great*, ed. Philip Schaff, Nicene and Post-Nicene Fathers (Buffalo, NY: Christian Literature, 1887–1894), second series, 8:48–49.

were obvious, and those being persecuted were obvious. The people became more numerous when warred against, and the blood of the martyrs, watering the churches, nurtured many more champions of piety, and those who came after stripped for combat with the zeal of their predecessors. Then we Christians had peace with one another, the peace that the Lord left to us, a peace that now not even a trace remains any longer with us, so cruelly have we driven it away from one another.

Hexaemeron 4.7

4.7. If the sea is beautiful and merits praise by God,[2] how much more beautiful is the gathering together of such a church in which the mingled sound (like some wave breaking upon the shore) of men, women, and children is sending up our petitions to God. A deep calm preserves it unmoved, since evil spirits are unable to trouble it with heretical doctrines.

2. Gen 1:10.

21

Gregory of Nyssa

Gregory was the younger brother of Basil the Great, who secured his appointment as bishop of Nyssa about 372, a position he held, although interrupted by an exile, until his death about 395. He is notable as a philosophical theologian and master of Christian spirituality.

In referring to the gifts acquired in Egypt that the Israelites brought to Moses for the construction of the tabernacle,[1] Gregory paid this tribute to his brother: "It is possible to see this happening even now. For many bring to the church of God their profane learning as a kind of gift: Such a man was the great Basil, who acquired the Egyptian wealth[2] in every respect during his youth and dedicated this wealth to God for the adornment of the church, the true tabernacle."[3] Gregory himself took his place in a long line of interpreters from Origen

1. Exod 35:4–9, 21–29.
2. I.e., pagan learning.
3. Gregory of Nyssa, *Life of Moses* 2.116.

forward who found analogies between the Israelite tabernacle according to Exodus and the Christian church. It is characteristic that he gives prominence to the ascetic life.

Life of Moses 2.184–87

2.184. Whenever the prophet [Moses] looks to the tabernacle above, he sees the heavenly realities through these symbols. But if one should look to the tabernacle below (since in many places the church also is called Christ by Paul),[4] it would be well to regard the names "apostles, teachers, and prophets" as referring to those servants of the divine mystery whom Scripture also calls pillars of the church.[5] . . . And again the divine apostle bids others to be pillars, saying "Be steadfast and immovable."[6] . . .

2.185. In this tabernacle, both the sacrifice of praise and the incense of prayer are seen offered continually at morning and evening. . . . When hearing about the lavers,[7] one will certainly perceive those who wash away the blemish of sins with mystical water.[8] . . .

2.186. The interconnecting courts that surround the tabernacle[9] are fittingly understood as the harmony, love, and peace of believers. . . .

2.187. The skin dyed red and the coverings made of hair,[10] which add to the decoration of the tabernacle, would be perceived respectively as the mortification of the sinful flesh (the figure of which is the skin dyed red) and the ascetic way

4. 1 Cor 12:12; Eph 1:23.
5. 1 Cor 12:28–29; Gal 2:9.
6. 1 Cor 15:58.
7. Exod 30:17; 38:8.
8. I.e., those who perform baptisms.
9. Exod 38:9–20.
10. Exod 26:1–10; 36:8–19.

of life. By these the tabernacle of the church is especially beautified. By nature these skins do not have in themselves a vital power, but they become bright red because of the red dye. This teaches that grace, which flourishes through the Spirit, is not found in persons unless they first make themselves dead to sin. . . . The woven hair, which produced a fabric rough and hard to the touch, foreshadows the self-control that is rough and consumes the habitual passions. The life of virginity demonstrates in itself all such things, as it chastises the flesh of all those who live this way.

22

Ephrem the Syrian

Ephrem (or Ephraem) lived from approximately 306 to 373. He was active at Nisibis and then Edessa, where he was a deacon and teacher in a school of biblical and theological studies. Ephrem is the classic author for all branches of Syriac-speaking Christianity. He wrote both prose and poetic works on a wide variety of religious themes, notable for their striking and beautiful imagery.

Ephrem, like his Western counterparts, viewed the church as a bride[1] and deplored the divisions occasioned by theological conflicts.[2] He developed the bridal imagery in several passages that present the church in succession to Israel in the Old Testament.[3] Our selection, from *Hymns on Paradise*, adds another dimension to the understanding of the nature of

1. *Hymns on Faith* 14.
2. *Hymns on Faith* 79.8–10.
3. Sebastian Brock, *The Luminous Eye* (Kalamazoo, MI: Cistercian Publications, 1985), 115–26.

church by bringing it into relation to the original Paradise, the Garden of Eden restored.

Hymns on Paradise 6.7–10

6.7. God planted the fair Garden,
He built the pure Church;
upon the Tree of Knowledge
He established the injunction.
He gave joy, but they took no delight,
He gave admonition, but they were unafraid.
In the Church He implanted
the Word
which causes rejoicing with its promises,
which causes fear with its warnings:
he who despises the Word, perishes,
he who takes warning, lives.
6.8. The assembly of saints
bears resemblance to Paradise:
in it each day is plucked
the fruit of Him who gives life to all;
in it, my brethren, is trodden
the cluster of grapes, to be the Medicine of Life.
. . .
6.9. Among the saints none is naked,
for they have put on glory,
nor is any clad in those leaves
or standing in shame,
for they have found, through our Lord,
the robe that belongs to Adam and Eve.
As the Church
purges her ears
of the serpent's poison,
those who had lost their garments,
having listened to it and become diseased,
have now been renewed and whitened.
6.10. . . .
The Creator saw the Church
and was pleased;
He resided in that Paradise
which she had planted for His honor,

just as He had planted the Garden
for her delight.[4]

4. Translation by Sebastian Brock, *Saint Ephrem: Hymns on Paradise*, Popular Patristics (Crestwood, NY: St. Vladimir's Seminary Press, 1990), 111–12.

23

Ambrose

After a successful career in civil administration, Ambrose was bishop of Milan from 374 to 397. He transmitted much of Eastern Christian theology to the West but also made important contributions of his own through numerous writings. In his work *On the Faith*, he expounded the Nicene faith on the Trinity and the incarnation. In the quotation below, Ambrose repeats the idea of the church as the bride of Christ, who is the mother of believers. As in Revelation 12, the mother includes God's people before the coming of Christ. In the subsequent sections, Ambrose continues the early Christian polemic on the exclusion of the synagogue from the life and joy of God's favor[1] and quotes from the Song of Songs as referring to Christ and his bride, the church.[2]

1. Ambrose, *On the Faith* 3.10.73.
2. Ibid., 3.10.74.

On the Faith 3.10.72

3.10.72. Christ alone, then, is the Bridegroom to whom the church, his bride, comes from the nations and gives herself in marriage. Previously she was poor and starving but is now rich with Christ's harvest. She gathers in the hidden bosom of her mind handfuls of the rich crop and gleanings of the Word that she may nourish with fresh food she who is worn out, bereaved by the death of her son, and starving, even the mother of the dead people. She does not leave the widow and destitute, while she seeks new children.[3]

3. Adapted from H. de Romestin, trans., *The Principal Works of St. Ambrose*, ed. Philip Schaff, Nicene and Post-Nicene Fathers (Buffalo, NY: Christian Literature, 1887–1894), second series, 10:253.

24

The Niceno-Constantinopolitan Creed of 381

The creed recited in many churches as the "Nicene Creed" is not the creed adopted at the first ecumenical council in Nicaea in 325 but the modified and expanded version of the creed approved at the second ecumenical council in Constantinople in 381. Hence, it is more properly called by the clumsy name Niceno-Constantinopolitan Creed. It has similarities to the creed of the Jerusalem church commented on by Cyril of Jerusalem in an earlier selection.

The first two articles confess faith in "the one God, Almighty Father" and "the one Lord Jesus Christ, the one and only Son of God." I quote the third article with its expanded statement about the Holy Spirit, which includes the church as part of the confession about the Holy Spirit. The words about the church give creedal affirmation to the four classic marks of the church: its unity, its sanctity, its universality, and its apostolicity in origin and doctrine. The phrase "one, holy, catholic, and apostolic church" as a description of the church has been subsequently often repeated and parts of this description have occurred in many of our selections.

Creed Approved by the Council of Constantinople, 381

[We believe] also in the Holy Spirit, the Lord and Giver of Life, who proceeds from the Father, who is worshiped and glorified together with the Father and the Son, who spoke through the prophets. In one, holy, catholic, and apostolic church. We confess one baptism for the forgiveness of sins. We await the resurrection of the dead and the life of the age to come. Amen.

25

John Chrysostom

John was given the name Chrysostom, "Golden Mouth," because of his preaching ability. He was a presbyter in Antioch of Syria from 386 to 398, during which time he preached the sermons on Ephesians, from which the selection below comes. Called to become bishop of Constantinople (398–407), he was caught up in the ecclesiastical politics of the time and its accompanying turmoil, for which he was unsuited. John Chrysostom set the standard for preaching in the Greek church. His homilies contain exposition of Scripture and timely application to his hearers. Our quotation sets forth the unity of the church as the body of Christ, composed of the faithful throughout the world in the past (before Christ's coming), the present, and the future.

Homilies on Ephesians 10.1

10.1. [Commenting on Eph 4:4.] What is the "one body"? The

faithful everywhere in the inhabited world, both those who are and are becoming and those who will be. Again, also, those who have been found faithful before the coming of Christ are one body. How so? Because those also saw Christ. [John 8:56; 5:46 quoted.] . . . We receive the body for unity even as with the one head. If there is one head, there is also one body.

26

Theodore of Mopsuestia

Theodore was bishop of Mopsuestia in Syria from 392 to 428. He was recognized as the preeminent exegete and theologian of the Church of the East ("Nestorian"); consequently, most of his works are preserved in Syriac. Theodore interpreted the Scriptures in a historical sense, but he found in the Old Testament types of the Christian dispensation. His work *On the Sacraments* along with the works of John Chrysostom reflect the practice and theology of the church at Antioch. Our quotation is taken from its chapter 2, part of his address to those preparing for baptism. In this passage, the church is presented as a symbol of heavenly things and as a new city where one is enrolled as a citizen at baptism.

On the Sacraments 2

2. [The Lord] will take us up and ascend into heaven where His Kingdom is seen and where all of us shall be with Him,

free and exempt from all troubles, in happiness and pleasure, and enjoying to the full the benefits of that kingdom. Those who draw nigh unto Him in this world He wished them to be, through religion and faith, as in the symbol of the heavenly things, and He so constituted the Church as to be a symbol of the heavenly things; and He wished that those who believe in Him should live in it. . . . [1 Tim 3:15 quoted.] Church "of the *living* God" means that His name is for ever and ever, and this demonstrates that the believers will enjoy life eternally, while the expression "pillar and ground of the truth" denotes that life firm, solid, unshakeable and unchangeable in which (the believer) will be seen and from which he will also receive his power.

He, therefore, who is desirous of drawing nigh unto baptism comes to the Church of God through which he expects to reach that life of the heavenly abode. He ought to think that he is coming to be the citizen of a new and great city, and he should, therefore, show great care in everything that is required of him before his enrolment in it.[1]

1. Translation by A. Mingana, *On the Sacraments*, in *Woodbrooke Studies*, ed. A. Mingana (Cambridge: Heffer & Sons, 1933), 6:24.

27

Augustine

Augustine was bishop of Hippo in North Africa from 395 to 430. He is a monumental transition figure: the climax of Latin patristic literature and the foundational thinker for the medieval Western church. His voluminous corpus of surviving works could provide a whole volume on the understanding of the church. Our selections from him provide a summary of points found in earlier writers and some of his distinctive emphases, but I have not felt it necessary to include passages referring to the common images of the church as body and bride of Christ (*Sermon* 341.1.1; 9.11).

In *On Faith and the Creed*, Augustine in explaining the article about the "holy catholic church" affirms that the catholic church is holy and universal. Augustine's predecessors in North Africa had argued that these characteristics provide the means of distinguishing it from heretics and schismatics. Heretics violate the command to love God supremely, and schismatics disobey the command to love the neighbor. Unacknowledged problems with this traditional claim are that Christianity at its beginning was considered a sect in Judaism, so this argument could have been used against it. Moreover, through history schismatic groups have sometimes recovered or advanced perspectives not recognized by the majority church.

Although earlier authors mainly used the language of the kingdom of God for the future kingdom, Augustine in *City of God* 20.9 stated that the church is the present reign of Christ. He denied Rev 20:1-6 to the premillennialists, arguing that the period of one thousand years refers symbolically to the period after the coming of Christ in which the saints share in the kingdom with Christ. Nevertheless, he could also say that the church included the righteous persons of the Old Testament.[1] Yet at other times Augustine marked the beginning of the church with Christ or at Jerusalem with the descent of the Holy Spirit.[2]

A realist as well as a creative thinker, Augustine recognized the mixed character of the church. In *On Catechizing the Uninstructed* 19.31, he refers to the presence of good and evil persons in the church. He employs an agricultural metaphor for the amount of chaff exceeding the amount of grain in order to keep inquirers from being discouraged by there being a greater number of sinners than godly persons. Augustine in this selection refers to the two communities, the two cities, which are the organizing principle in his great work the *City of God*. He later adds that although the perverse may find their way into the church, they cannot find their way into the

1. Augustine, *Sermon* 4.11; *On Catechizing the Uninstructed* 3.6.
2. Augustine, *City of God* 18.54, for the Christian religion beginning with the events in Acts 2.

kingdom of heaven.[3] The mixed character of the church had its precedent in Israel, which was a figure of the church.[4]

The city of God and the city of the world are two societies issuing from two kinds of love.[5] The church is a community of divine love. The image of the church as mother, which came so naturally to Latin Christians but others as well, is frequent in Augustine. As a mother, the church teaches the various classes of persons in its membership.[6] Christians are children of God the Father and of the church the mother, who gives birth to new members.[7]

The work usually translated literally as *On Christian Doctrine* would be better translated as *On Christian Teaching* or *On Christian Instruction* in order to bring out the active meaning appropriate to the content of the treatise. The authority of the church, especially in disciplinary matters, is shown by the keys of the kingdom given to it.[8]

In commenting on the prophet Haggai, Augustine states that the restored temple is the church built by Christ.[9] The church as the new temple built of "living stones" (people) shows its continuity with the institutions of the old covenant but also its superiority to them.

The *Enchiridion*, or *Handbook on Faith, Hope, and Charity*, devotes most of its content to faith (an exposition of the articles of the creed) with briefer attention to hope (the Lord's Prayer) and charity (love for God and neighbor). Augustine relates the church to other Christian doctrines. For instance, the church is the temple of the Trinity. It contains not only the

3. Augustine, *On Catechizing the Uninstructed* 27.55.
4. Ibid., 19.33.
5. Augustine, *City of God* 14.28.
6. Augustine, *Way of Life of the Catholic Church* 30.62–63.
7. Augustine, *Sermon* 216.7.
8. Augustine, *On Christian Doctrine* 1.22.18.
9. Augustine, *City of God* 18.48.

saved on earth but also the angels in heaven, both of which groups have the task of worshiping God.[10]

Picking up on emphases of his predecessors in North African Christianity, notably Cyprian, Augustine says that outside the church one does not have the Holy Spirit (*Letter* 185.50); hence, outside the church there is no salvation (*On Baptism* 4.17.24). Augustine's canon of the Old Testament included the Wisdom of Solomon (cited in the quotation as Wis).

Within the church, the saints exercise the gifts of the Spirit (*Sermon* 267.4). These are as varied as the functions of parts of a human body. Being alive with the Spirit requires holding on to the virtues associated with the Spirit.

On Faith and the Creed 9.21–10.21

9.21. Inasmuch as love is enjoined upon us, not only toward God, when it was said, "You shall love the Lord your God with all your heart, and with all your soul, and with all your mind,"[11] but also toward our neighbor, "for you shall love," he says, "your neighbor as yourself";[12] and inasmuch, moreover, as the faith in question is less fruitful, if it does not comprehend a congregation and society of human beings wherein brotherly love may operate; 10.21. inasmuch, I repeat, as this is the case, we believe also in the "holy church," assuredly the "catholic" church. For both heretics and schismatics style their congregations churches. But heretics, in holding false opinions regarding God, do injury to the faith itself; while schismatics, on the other hand, in wicked separations break off from brotherly love, although they may believe just what we believe. Wherefore neither do the heretics belong to the church

10. Augustine, *Enchiridion* 15.56.
11. Deut 6:5.
12. Luke 10:27.

catholic, which loves God, nor do the schismatics form a part of the same, inasmuch as the church loves the neighbor, and consequently readily forgives the neighbor's sins, because it prays that forgiveness may be extended to itself by him who has reconciled us to himself, doing away with all past things, and calling us to a new life. And until we reach the perfection of this new life, we cannot be without sins.[13]

City of God 20.9

20.9. In the interim, while the devil is bound for a thousand years, the saints reign with Christ, also for a thousand years;[14] and these thousand years are no doubt to be understood in the same way, that is, as the time since Christ's first coming. This reign is, of course, quite different from the kingdom of which Christ will say at the end . . . [Matt 25:34 quoted]. But his saints—to whom he says, *Behold I am with you until the end of the world*[15]—are reigning with him even now, although in another and far lesser sense. If this were not so, the Church obviously would not be called his kingdom, or the kingdom of heaven, here and now in the present. [Augustine proceeds to quote passages in which the kingdom refers to the church—Matt 13:52; 13:39–41; 5:19] . . . Accordingly, the Church as it is now includes both sorts of people; but, when only the second sort [those who do what they teach] is included, that is the Church as it will be when there are no evil persons in it.

Even now, therefore, the Church is the kingdom of Christ and the kingdom of heaven, and so even now the saints reign with him, although not in the same sense in which they will

13. Adapted from S. D. F. Salmond, trans., *Augustine: On the Holy Trinity, Doctrinal Treatises, Moral Treatises*, ed. Philip Schaff, Nicene and Post-Nicene Fathers (Buffalo, NY: Christian Literature, 1887), first series, 3:331.
14. Rev 20:4.
15. Matt 28:20.

ultimately reign. . . . In short, the ones who reign with him are the ones who are in his kingdom in such a way that they themselves are his kingdom. . . .

It is about this kingdom at war, then, that The Apocalypse is speaking in the passage which we are considering. It is there that there is still conflict with the enemy, and there that we sometimes battle against the vices when they oppose us and sometimes rule them when they yield to us, until we come to that most peaceful kingdom where we shall reign without any enemy. . . . [Rev 20:4 quoted.] No one should think that this refers to the last judgment. Rather, we should understand that it refers to the thrones of the leaders and to the leaders themselves by whom the Church is now governed. . . .

. . . [Rev 20:4] He is speaking about the souls of the martyrs whose bodies have not yet been restored to them. For the souls of the devout dead are not separated from the Church, which is even now the kingdom of Christ. . . . Thus the Church now first reigns with Christ in both the living and the dead.[16]

Sermon 4.11

4.11. [Commenting on the story of Isaac blessing Esau and Jacob, interpreted as the Jews, the older people, and Christians, the younger people, respectively—Genesis 27] [Isaac] wants to bless the elder [son], because the old testament was making promises to the first people. It addresses promises to none but the Jews. They are the ones it seems to make promises to, to them it seems to promise everything. They are called out of Egypt, liberated from their enemies, led through the sea, fed on manna, given the testament, given the law, given the

16. Translation by William Babcock, *The City of God* [De Civitate Dei] *XI–XXII*, The Works of Saint Augustine: A Translation for the 21st Century I/7 (Hyde Park, NY: New City, 2013), 405–7. Used by permission.

promises, given the promised land itself. No wonder that he wanted to bless his elder son! But in the guise of the elder it is the younger who gets blessed. For the mother [Rebekah] fills the role of the Church. Now by Church, brothers, you must understand not only those who began to be saints after the Lord's advent and nativity, but all who have ever been saints belong to the same Church. You can't say that our father Abraham does not belong to us, just because he lived before Christ was born of the virgin, and we have become Christians such a long time afterward, that is after Christ's passion; after all, the apostle says that we are *the children of Abraham*[17] by imitating Abraham's faith. If then we are admitted to the Church by imitating him, are we going to exclude the man himself from the Church? It is this Church that was represented by Rebecca the wife of Isaac. It was this Church that was also to be found in the holy prophets who understood the old testament, realizing that its material promises signified something or other spiritual. If it was spiritual, then all spiritual people belong to the younger son, because first comes the material one and afterward the spiritual.[18]

On Catechizing the Uninstructed 19.31, 33

19.31. Neither ought we to be moved by the consideration that many consent to the devil and few follow God; for the grain, too, in comparison with the chaff has greatly the defect in number. But even as the farmer knows what to do with the mighty heap of chaff, so the multitude of sinners is nothing to God, who knows what to do with them, so as not to let the administration of his kingdom be disordered and dishonored

17. Gal 3:7.
18. Translation by Edmund Hill, *Sermons I*, Works of Saint Augustine: A Translation for the 21st Century III/1 (Hyde Park, NY: New City, 1990), 191.

in any part. Nor is the devil to be supposed to have proved victorious for the mere reason of his drawing away with him more than the few by whom he may be overcome. In this way there are two communities—one of the ungodly, and another of the holy—which are at present commingled in respect of bodies, but separated in respect of wills, and which, moreover, are destined to be separated also in respect of bodily presence in the day of judgment. For all persons who love pride and temporal power with vain elation and pomp of arrogance, and all spirits who set their affections on such things and seek their own glory in the subjection of others are bound fast together in one association. . . . And, again, all persons and all spirits who humbly seek the glory of God and not their own, and who follow him in piety, belong to one fellowship. . . .

19.33. . . . Of Abraham was born a people, by whom the one true God who made heaven and earth should be worshiped when all other nations did service to idols and evil spirits. In that people, plainly, the future church was much more evidently prefigured. For in it there was a carnal multitude that worshiped God with a view to visible benefits. But in it there were also a few who thought of the future rest and looked longingly for the heavenly fatherland. . . . They constituted a prophecy of this time, at which the church is being gathered together out of all nations through faith in the passion of Christ. . . . In all these [benefits and chastisements experienced by Israel], nevertheless, there were also spiritual mysteries signified, such as were meant to bear upon Christ and the church. Of this church those saints also were members, although they existed in this life previous to the birth of Christ, the Lord, according to the flesh.[19]

19. Adapted from Salmond, *Augustine: On the Holy Trinity, Doctrinal Treatises, Moral Treatises*, 303.

Way of Life of the Catholic Church 30.62–63

30.62. For to Christians this rule of life is given, that we should love the Lord our God with all the heart, with all the soul, and with all the mind, and our neighbor as ourselves; for on these two commandments hang all the Law and the Prophets.[20] Rightly, then, Catholic church, most true mother of Christians, do you teach that God alone, to find whom is the happiest life, must be worshiped in perfect purity and chastity, bringing in no creature as an object of adoration whom we should be required to serve. . . .

30.63. Your [the Catholic church's] training and teaching are childlike for children, forcible for youths, peaceful for the aged, taking into account the age of the mind as well as of the body. You subject women to their husbands in chaste and faithful obedience, not to gratify passion, but for the propagation of offspring and for domestic society. You give to men authority over their wives, not to mock the weaker sex, but in the laws of unfeigned love. You subordinate children to their parents in a kind of free bondage, and you set parents over their children in a godly rule. You bind brothers to brothers in a religious tie stronger and closer than that of blood. . . . You teach servants to cleave to their masters from delight in their task rather than from the necessity of their position. You render masters forbearing to the servants, from a regard to God their common Master, and more disposed to advise than to compel. You unite citizen to citizen, nation to nation, yes person to person from the recollection of their first parents, not only in society but also in fraternity. You teach kings to seek the good of their peoples; you counsel peoples to be subject to their kings. You teach carefully to whom honor

20. Matt 22:36–40.

is due, to whom regard, to whom reverence, to whom fear, to whom consolation, to whom admonition, to whom encouragement, to whom discipline, to whom rebuke, to whom punishment; showing both how all are not due to all, and how to all love is due, and how injury is due to none.[21]

On Christian Doctrine 1.22.18

1.22.18. Christ has given, therefore, the keys to his church, that whatever it should bind on earth might be bound in heaven, and whatever it should loose on earth might be loosed in heaven.[22] That is to say, that whoever in the church should not believe that his sins are remitted, they should not be remitted to him. But whoever should believe, and should repent, and turn from his sins, should be saved by the same faith and repentance on the ground of which he is received into the bosom of the church.[23]

City of God 18.48

18.48. This house of God [the church] is of greater glory than was that former house built of wood and stone and other precious materials and metals. Thus the prophecy of Haggai[24] was not fulfilled by the rebuilding of that former Temple. For that Temple can never be shown to have had as much glory after it was rebuilt as it had in the time of Solomon. On the contrary, the diminished glory of that house is shown first

21. Adapted from Richard Stothert, trans., *Augustine: The Anti-Manichaean Writings, The Anti-Donatist Writings*, ed. Philip Schaff, Nicene and Post-Nicene Fathers (Buffalo, NY: Christian Literature, 1887), first series, 4:58.
22. Matt 18:18.
23. Adapted from J. F. Shaw, trans., *Augustine: The City of God, Christian Doctrine*, ed. Philip Schaff, Nicene and Post-Nicene Fathers (Buffalo, NY: Christian Literature, 1886), first series, 2:27.
24. Hag 2:9.

by the cessation of prophecy and then the terrible disasters that came upon the people themselves, right down to the final destruction inflicted by the Romans. . . . But this house, which belongs to the new covenant, is certainly of greater glory, in that *living stones*[25] are better. For it is built of people, who believe and have been made new. It was signified by the rebuilding of that former Temple, however, because the rebuilding of that Temple itself signified by prophetic discourse another covenant, which is called the new covenant. Thus, when God said, through the prophet just mentioned, *And I will give peace in this place*,[26] we should understand the word *place* stands for that which it signifies. And so, because what was rebuilt in that place signified the Church, which was going to be built through Christ, we should take *I will give peace in this place* to mean nothing other than "I will give peace in the place which this place signifies."[27]

Enchiridion 15.56

15.56. Hence, the correct sequence of the Creed demanded that the Church be subjoined to the Trinity, as a dwelling to its Inhabitant, as a temple to God, and a city to its Founder. And here it is the whole Church that is to be understood—not that part only which sojourns on earth, praising the name of the Lord from the rising of the sun to its setting and chanting a new song of deliverance from its ancient captivity; but that part also which always was in heaven, which always remained loyal to God, its Creator, and did not experience the woe that springs from a fall. This part, consisting of the holy angels,

25. 1 Pet 2:5.
26. Hag 2:9.
27. Translation by William Babcock, *The City of God* [De Civitate Dei] *XI–XXII*, The Works of Saint Augustine: A Translation for the 21st Century I/7 (Hyde Park, NY: New City, 2013), 334. Used by permission.

abides in perpetual bliss and helps, as it should, the other part which is still in exile; for both parts will be one in the fellowship of eternity, and even now are one in the bond of charity, the whole Church having been instituted for the purpose of worshiping God. . . . Therefore, the temple of God, that is, of the sublime Trinity as a whole, is the Holy Church—the Church everywhere, in heaven and on earth.[28]

Letter 185.50

185.50. Hence the Catholic Church alone is the body of Christ, and its head is the savior of his body.[29] The Holy Spirit gives life to no one outside this body, because, as the apostle himself says, *The love of God has been poured out in our hearts by the Holy Spirit who has been given to us.*[30] But one who is an enemy of unity has no share in the love of God. Those, therefore, who are outside the Church do not have the Holy Spirit. Of them scripture itself says, *Those who keep themselves separate are merely natural and do not have the Spirit.*[31] But one who is in the Church only as a pretense does not receive the Spirit, because scripture says of such a person, *For the Holy Spirit of discipline will flee from a hypocrite.*[32] One who wants to have the Holy Spirit, therefore, should avoid remaining outside the Church and should avoid entering her as a pretense, or, if he has entered her in that way, he should avoid remaining in that pretense so that he may truly grow in union with the tree of life.[33]

28. Translation by Louis A. Arand, *St. Augustine: Faith Hope and Charity*, Ancient Christian Writers 3 (Westminster, MD: Newman Press, 1955), 59–60.
29. Eph 5:23.
30. Rom 5:5.
31. Jude 19.
32. Wis 1:5.
33. Translation by Roland Teske, *Letters 156–210*, Works of Saint Augustine: A Translation for the 21st Century II/3 (Hyde Park, NY: New City, 2004), 206.

Sermon 267.4

267.4. So none of you must say, "I have received the Holy Spirit; why aren't I speaking with the tongues of all the nations?" If you want to have the Holy Spirit, consider this, my dear brothers and sisters: our spirit, by which every person lives, is called the soul. And you can see what the soul does in the body. It quickens all its parts; it sees through the eyes, hears through the ears, smells through the nostrils, speaks with the tongue, works with the hands, walks with the feet. It's present simultaneously to all the body's parts, to make them alive; it gives life to all, their functions to each. The eye doesn't hear, the ear doesn't see, the tongue doesn't see, nor do ear and eye speak. But they're alive, all the same; the ear's alive, the tongue's alive; different functions, life in common.

That's what the Church of God is like: in some of the saints it works miracles, in other saints it proclaims the truth, in other saints it preserves virginity, in other saints it preserves married chastity; in some this, in others that. All doing their own thing, but living the same life together. In fact, what the soul is to the human body, the Holy Spirit is to the body of Christ, which is the Church. The Holy Spirit does in the whole Church what the soul does in all the parts of one body. But notice what you should beware of, see what you should notice, notice what you should be afraid of. It can happen in the human body—or rather from the body—that one part is cut off, a hand, a finger, a foot; does the soul follow the amputated part? When it was in the body, it was alive, cut off, it loses life. In the same way too Christian men and women are Catholics, while they are alive in the body; cut off, they have become heretics, the Spirit doesn't follow the amputated part. So if you wish to be alive with the Holy Spirit, hold on to loving-kindness, love truthfulness, long for oneness, that you may attain to everlastingness. Amen.[34]

34. Translation by Edmund Hill, *Sermons*, Works of Saint Augustine: A Translation for the 21st Century III/7 (New Rochelle, NY: New City, 1993), 276.

Bibliography

Primary Sources

Ambrose. *On the Faith*. In *De Fide*. Edited by O. Faller. Corpus scriptorum ecclesiasticorum latinorum 78. Vienna: Hölder-Pichler-Tempsky, 1962.

Apostolic Fathers: *1 Clement*, *2 Clement*, Ignatius of Antioch, Hermas. In Michael W. Holmes, ed. *The Apostolic Fathers: Greek Texts and English Translations*. 3rd ed. Grand Rapids: Baker Academic, 2007.

Athanasius. *Festal Letters*. In *Patrologia Cursus Completus*. Series Graeca 26. Edited by J.-P. Migne. Paris, 1857–1866.

____. *History of the Arians*. In *Athanasius Werke*. Vol. 3. Edited by H. G. Opitz. Berlin: de Gruyter, 1934.

Augustine. *On Faith and the Creed*; *City of God*; *Sermons*; *On Catechizing the Uninstructed*; *Way of Life of the Catholic Church*; *On Christian Doctrine*; *Enchiridion*; *Letters*. In The Works of Saint Augustine: A Translation for the 21st Century. Edited by John Rotelle et al. Hyde Park, NY: New City, 1990–.

Basil the Great. *Hexaemeron*. In *Homélies sur l'Hexaéméron*. Edited by S. Giet. 2nd ed. Sources chrétiennes 26. Paris: Cerf, 1968.

____. *Letters*. In *Saint Basil: The Letters*. Edited by R. J. Deferrari. 4 vols.

Loeb Classical Library. Cambridge, MA: Harvard University Press, 1961–1964.

____. *On the Holy Spirit. Sur le Saint-Esprit*. Edited by B. Pruche. Rev. ed. Sources chrétiennes 17. Paris: Cerf, 1968.

Clement of Alexandria. *Exhortation to the Greeks; Instructor; Miscellanies*. In Die griechischen christlichen Schriftsteller der ersten drei Jahrhunderte 15, 17, 39. Edited by Otto Stählin. Leipzig: Hinrichs, 1905–1936.

Cyprian. *On the Unity of the Catholic Church*. In *De lapsis* and *De ecclesiae catholicae unitate*. Edited by M. Bévenot. Oxford Early Christian Texts. Oxford: Clarendon, 1971.

Cyril of Jerusalem. *Catechetical Lectures*. In *Patrologia Cursus Completus*. Series Graeca 33. Edited by J.-P. Migne. Paris, 1857–1866.

Ephrem the Syrian. *Saint Ephrem: Hymns on Paradise*. Translated by Sebastian Brock. Popular Patristics. Crestwood, NY: St. Vladimir's Seminary Press, 1990.

Eusebius. *Church History* (including *Letter of the Churches of Vienne and Lyons*). In *The Ecclesiastical History*. Edited by K. Lake and J. E. L. Oulton. 2 vols. Loeb Classical Library. Cambridge, MA: Harvard University Press, 1926–1932.

____. *Preparation for the Gospel*. In *Eusebius Werke*. Vol. 8/1–2. Edited by K. Mras and É. des Places. 2nd ed. Die griechischen christlichen Schriftsteller der ersten drei Jahrhunderte. Berlin: Akademie, 1982–1983.

Firmilian. *Letter to Cyprian*. In *Epistularium*. Edited by G. F. Diercks. Corpus Christianorum Series Latina 3B. Turnhout: Brepols, 1994.

Gregory of Nyssa. *Life of Moses*. In *Gregorii Nysseni, De Vita Moysis*. Edited by H. Musurillo. Gregorii Nysseni Opera 7.1. Leiden: Brill, 1964.

Hippolytus. *On Christ and Antichrist*. In Biblioteca patristica 10. Edited by E. Norelli. Florence: Dehoniane, 1987.

Irenaeus. *Against Heresies*. In *Contre les hérésies*. Edited by A. Rousseau et al. Sources chrétiennes 100, 152, 153, 210, 211, 163, 264, 293, 294. Paris: Cerf, 1965–1982.

John Chrysostom. *Homilies on Ephesians*. In *Patrologia Cursus Completus*. Series Graeca 62. Edited by J.-P. Migne. Paris, 1857–1866.

Justin Martyr. *Dialogue with Trypho*. In *Dialogus cum Tryphone*. Edited by M. Marcovich. Patristische Texte und Studien 47. Berlin: de Gruyter, 1997.

Methodius. *Banquet*. In *Symposium*. Edited by H. Musurillo. Sources chrétiennes 95. Paris: Cerf, 1963.

Niceno-Constantinopolitan Creed. In *Enchiridion Symbolorum*. Edited by H. Denzinger and A. Schönmetzer. 32nd ed. Freiburg: Herder, 1963.

Origen. *Against Celsus*. In *Contre Celse*. Edited by M. Borret. Sources chrétiennes 132, 136, 147, 150, 227. Paris: Cerf, 1967–1976.

____. *Commentary on John*. In *Commentaire sur saint Jean*. Edited by C. Blanc. Sources chrétiennes 120, 157, 222, 290, 385. Paris: Cerf, 1964–1992.

____. *Commentary on Matthew*. In *Origenes Werke*. Edited by E. Klostermann et al. Die griechischen christlichen Schriftsteller der ersten drei Jahrhunderte 38, 40, 41. Leipzig: Hinrichs, 1935–1955.

____. *Commentary on Song of Songs*. In *Commentaire sur le Cantique des cantiques*. Edited by L. Brésard et al. Sources chrétiennes 375–76. Paris: Cerf, 1991–1992.

____. *Homilies on Exodus*. In *Homiliae in Exodum*. Edited by M. Borret. Sources chrétiennes 321. Paris: Cerf, 1985.

____. *Homilies on Luke*. *Homélies sur S. Luc*. Edited by H. Crouzel et al. Sources chrétiennes 87. Paris: Cerf, 1962.

Pseudo-Clement. *Letter to James*. In *Pseudo-Clementines*. Edited by J. N. Bremmer. Leuven: Peeters, 2010.

Tertullian. *Apology; On Repentance; On Modesty; On Prescription against Heretics; Exhortation to Chastity; Against the Jews; On the Soul*. In Corpus Christianorum Series Latina 1, 2. Turnhout: Brepols, 1954.

Theodore of Mopsuestia. *On the Sacraments.* In *Woodbrooke Studies.* Edited by A. Mingana. Vol. 6. Cambridge: Heffer & Sons, 1933.

Secondary Sources: Translations

Arand, Louis A., ed. *St. Augustine: Faith Hope and Charity.* Ancient Christian Writers 3. Westminster, MD: Newman Press, 1955.

Babcock, William, trans. *The City of God [*De Civitate Dei*] XI–XXII.* The Works of Saint Augustine: A Translation for the 21st Century I/7. Hyde Park, NY: New City, 2013.

Brock, Sebastian, trans. *Saint Ephrem: Hymns on Paradise.* Popular Patristics. Crestwood, NY: St. Vladimir's Seminary Press, 1990.

De Romestin, H., trans. *The Principal Works of St. Ambrose.* Edited by Philip Schaff. Nicene and Post-Nicene Fathers, Second Series, Volume 10. Buffalo, NY: Christian Literature, 1887–1894.

Falls, Thomas. *Writings of Saint Justin Martyr: First Apology.* Fathers of the Church. Washington, DC: Catholic University of America Press, 1948.

Hill, Edmund. *Sermons.* Works of Saint Augustine: A Translation for the 21st Century III/1, 7. Hyde Park, NY: New City, 1990.

Holmes, Michael W., ed. *The Apostolic Fathers: Greek Texts and English Translations.* 3rd ed. Grand Rapids: Baker Academic, 2007.

Jackson, Blomfield, trans. *The Treatise* De Spiritu Sancto, *the Nine Homilies of the Hexaemeron, and the Letters of Saint Basil the Great.* Edited by Philip Schaff. Nicene and Post-Nicene Fathers, Second Series, Volume 8. Buffalo, NY: Christian Literature, 1887–1894.

Lawson, R. P., trans. *Origen: The Song of Songs: Commentary and Homilies.* Ancient Christian Writers 26. Westminster, MD: Newman Press, 1957.

Mingana, A. *Woodbrooke Studies.* Volume 6. Cambridge: Heffer & Sons, 1933.

Robertson, Archibald, trans. *Select Writings and Letters of Athanasius,*

Bishop of Alexandria. Nicene and Post-Nicene Fathers, Second Series, Volume 4. Buffalo, NY: Christian Literature, 1887–1894.

Salmond, S. D. F., trans. *Augustine: On the Holy Trinity, Doctrinal Treatises, Moral Treatises.* Nicene and Post-Nicene Fathers, First Series, Volume 3. Buffalo, NY: Christian Literature, 1887.

Shaw, J. F., trans. *Augustine: The City of God, Christian Doctrine.* Nicene and Post-Nicene Fathers, First Series, Volume 2. Buffalo, NY: Christian Literature, 1886.

Stothert, Richard, trans. *Augustine: The Anti-Manichaean Writings, The Anti-Donatist Writings.* Nicene and Post-Nicene Fathers, First Series, Volume 4. Buffalo, NY: Christian Literature, 1887.

Teske, Roland. *Letters 156–210.* Works of Saint Augustine: A Translation for the 21st Century II/3. Hyde Park, NY: New City, 2004.

Wallis, Ernest, trans. *Fathers of the Third Century: Hippolytus, Cyprian, Caius, Novatian, Appendix.* Edited by Alexander Roberts and James Donaldson. Volume 5. The Ante-Nicene Fathers. Buffalo, NY: Christian Literature, 1885–1896.

Secondary Sources: Works

Bardy, Gustav. *La théologie de l'Église de Clément de Rom au saint Irénée.* Paris: Cerf, 1945.

____. *La théologie de l'Église de saint Irénée au concile de Nicée.* Paris: Cerf, 1947.

Brock, Sebastian, trans. *The Luminous Eye: The Spiritual World Vision of Saint Ephrem the Syrian* . Kalamazoo, MI: Cistercian, 1985.

Buell, D. K. *Why This New Race: Ethnic Reasoning in Early Christianity.* New York: Columbia University Press, 2005.

Christo, G. G. *The Church's Identity Established through Images according to Saint John Chrysostom.* Rolli, NH: Orthodox Research Institute, 2006.

Dulles, Avery. *Models of the Church.* Garden City, NY: Doubleday, 1987.

Ferguson, Everett. *The Church of Christ: A Biblical Ecclesiology for Today.* Grand Rapids: Eerdmans, 1996.

____. *The Early Church at Work and Worship.* Vol. 1, *Ministry, Ordination, Covenant, and Canon.* Eugene, OR: Cascade, 2013.

Halton, Thomas. *The Church.* Message of the Fathers of the Church 3. Wilmington, DE: Michael Glazier, 1985.

Hinson, E. Glenn. *Understandings of the Church.* Sources of Early Christian Thought. Philadelphia: Fortress Press, 1986.

Ledegang, F. *Mysterium Ecclesiae: Images of the Church and its Members in Origen.* Leuven: Leuven University Press, 2001.

Minear, Paul. *Images of the Church in the New Testament.* Philadelphia: Westminster, 1960.

Peterson, Erik. "Das Schiff als Symbol der Kirche: Die Tat des Messias im eschatologischen Meerssturm in der jüdischen und altchristlichen Ueberlieferung." *Theologische Zeitschrift* 6 (1950): 77–79.

Plumpe, Joseph C. *Mater Ecclesia: An Inquiry into the Concept of the Church as Mother in Early Christianity.* Washington, DC: Catholic University of America Press, 1943.

Rahner, Hugo. *Symbole der Kirche: Die Ekklesiologie der Väter.* Salzburg: Otto Müller, 1964.

Rankin, David. *Tertullian and the Church.* Cambridge: Cambridge University Press, 1995.

Rikhof, H. *The Concept of the Church: A Methodological Inquiry into the Use of Metaphor in Ecclesiology.* London: Sheed & Ward, 1981.

Spikowski, Ladislas. *La doctrin de l'Église dans Saint Irénée.* Strasbourg: Université de Strasbourg, 1926.

Index of Scripture

Index of Patristics

Index of Names and Subjects